P9-DCX-891

Stop the Meeting I Want to Get Off

HOW TO ELIMINATE ENDLESS MEETINGS WHILE IMPROVING YOUR TEAM'S COMMUNICATION, PRODUCTIVITY, AND EFFECTIVENESS

SCOTT SNAIR

McGRAW-HILL

New York   Chicago   San Francisco   Lisbon   London
Madrid   Mexico City   Milan   New Delhi   San Juan
Seoul   Singapore   Sydney   Toronto

1 2 3 4 5 6 7 8 9 0   DOC/DOC   0 9 8 7 6 5 4 3

ISBN 0-07-141106-2

This publication is designed to provide accurate and authoritative information in regard to the subject matter covered. It is sold with the understanding that neither the author nor the publisher is engaged in rendering legal, accounting, or other professional service. If legal advice or other expert assistance is required, the services of a competent professional person should be sought.

—From a declaration of principles jointly adopted by a committee
of the American Bar Association and a committee of publishers

This book is printed on recycled, acid-free paper containing a minimum of 50% recycled de-inked fiber.

McGraw-Hill books are available at special quantity discounts to use as premiums and sales promotions, or for use in corporate training programs. For more information, please write to the Director of Special Sales, Professional Publishing, McGraw-Hill, Two Penn Plaza, New York, NY 10121-2298. Or contact your local bookstore.

FOR PATTI AND KATIE

Contents

Acknowledgments

Many thanks to the influential leaders I have known and learned from over the years, especially John Barry, Alan Shephard, Bailey Trueman, John Jeppi, Roger Vaughan, John Schotzko, Karl Stebbins, Freddy McFarren, Karen Barry, and John Pastor.

I appreciate the education professionals who have made my study of leadership—particularly business leadership—an important academic endeavor, especially Esther Taitsman, Sonja Eveslage, and Nancy Bailey.

I am deeply grateful to my editor, Mary Glenn, whose care and skilled counsel made me always eager to please. Her straightforward thoughts on style, structure, and the presentation of information were invaluable.

And a very special thank you to my literary agent, James C. Vines, who not only shared my enthusiasm for this specific project but who has pointed me, several times, in the right creative direction.

As with any earnest undertaking, this work inevitably became a family affair. My wife, Mary-Jane Snair, is a professional counselor who helped me to understand the way the human mind thinks. My sister, Patricia Snair Koski, is a long-time author of speech and language workbooks who offered me sound advice on finding a wider audience for my management concepts. And my brother, Andrew Snair, is a successful commercial artist with a clever imagination that I tapped more than once. I value your support.

And speaking of family, many thanks to my parents, Joseph and Lucille—continual sources of leadership and wisdom.

Introduction

From Ground Attack to Corporate Combat

A few times in my life, I have enjoyed watching extraordinary and effective leaders at work.

In 1991, three years after graduation from the U.S. Military Academy, I served in the Army as a cannon platoon leader. I had the honor of taking 70 soldiers 100 miles into Iraq during a ground attack and setting up a fire base there for a month. My commander throughout Operation Desert Storm was Captain Karl T. Stebbins.

Stebbins displayed a reassuring calm throughout our mission, walking the gun line and checking his sergeants and soldiers. By all accounts, his unit was admirably prepared, with each soldier knowing exactly what was expected of him in a complicated orchestration of moving, shooting, and communicating.

Remarkable, however, was that during the six months we had practiced in the Saudi Arabian desert for this mission, Stebbins had not brought the unit together for a meeting more than once! While other commanders had labored endlessly with their troops over huge charts and map display boards, Stebbins had concentrated on spending one-on-one time with his lieutenants, his platoon sergeants, and his gunnery sergeants—pulling out a small, folded map or using a stick in the sand when tactics needed discussion. We, in turn, followed suit, spending time with our soldiers, gun section by gun section—sometimes soldier by soldier—to ensure that each individual understood his unique role in accomplishing this important assignment.

Stebbins was always accessible, always close at hand. When enemy cannon rounds landed near my platoon, it was the captain, unruffled and almost serene, that reported the volleys over his radio—leading to the eventual detection and annihilation of their source. He was someone people respected and worked hard to please.

Fast-forward nearly 10 years. I was fighting yet another battle.

Having been out of the Army for years, I was working as a manufacturing and logistics manager for an international paper company. I had just informed all concerned at the mill that a desperate customer was about to get only half of the 40,000 pounds of paper he was expecting. The shipping coordinator was confirming the short inventory on her computer.

John Pastor, the head of planning and purchasing—and my boss—entered the shipping office with his trademark composure. "Everything we need for that order is here."

I looked at him incredulously. "You've got to be kidding."

He showed me his notepad. "I spoke with Quality. They have rechecked the five pallets in the Hold Product area—they're fine and just need data entry into inventory. I spoke with the shippers. They managed to find three pallets that had been repackaged but not re-entered into inventory. And I took a walk through the partials area myself. There are four half-skids that we can combine into two full ones. That's 10, plus the 10 on inventory. There's your order."

I looked at the figures, my mouth hanging open.

Over the years, Pastor had been asked to take on the simultaneous management of four different departments at our plant, each located as far away from the other three as geographically possible. Holding at least one staff meeting each day with his four department, managers (including me) would have been acceptable, standard fare. But Pastor was rarely one for meetings. Instead, he chose to walk the mill, talking with his managers, inspecting their departments, and chatting with their workers. He was both a methodical and motivating supervisor.

These two leaders serve as appropriate bookends for the 10 years I have spent observing, interviewing, and documenting dozens of innovative managers, both inside and outside my personal backdrops. As a West Pointer, a manager, and a college business instructor, I find the study of transformational leadership truly inspiring.

What common quality did I discover among these special men and women? They chose successful one-on-one communication, delegating, and a strong, hands-on style over staff meetings and work team conferences.

To put it bluntly, great managers do not hold business meetings. They have figured out a way to be successful without them.

I have formalized these attributes and actions into a system of meetingless management, and I have used it myself for years. These techniques, including something I call *organizational channeling*, are provided in this book. The steps are easy to follow, and the commentary regarding the uselessness of meetings is easy to digest. Each of the book's 10 parts stands alone as a lesson, and each three- or four-page subchapter can be read and pondered as a separate dose.

My primary desire in writing this book is to change the way all types of managers view the standard workplace meeting and to encourage them to replace their meetings with more results-directed and time-efficient ways of getting things done.

While I provide solid ideas in the text for avoiding the conferences of others, most of my instruction concentrates on offering the manager most likely to convene meetings convincing reasons and methods for not doing so. Why? Because no matter how much people may hate staff meetings, if their boss calls one, people will be there. The appreciation for fewer (or zero) meetings must begin with a team's manager. Therefore, my second hope in writing this book is to begin a valuable discussion among business leaders on whether or not a corporate culture so addicted to meetings is good for business itself.

Imagine a workday free from meetings. How much more could you accomplish? What great things could you go off and achieve? Perhaps after reading this text, the notion will not seem so far-fetched to you or your team.

Scott Snair

CHAPTER 1

Stop Surrendering to Meetings

ACCEPT YOUR DISTASTE FOR MEETINGS

Business meetings have taken over my life.

I am a young, midlevel manager who came to this company a few years ago hoping to be successful and make a difference. These days, most of what I do is count minutes at meetings.

Allow me to describe my average workday. I wake up at 5:30 A.M., following the lead of Benjamin Franklin. With everyone else asleep, I sit down with a cup of coffee and ponder my personal and professional goals for the day ahead. I jot down these goals, prioritize them, and schedule them in my daily planner. I still have time to make an entry or two into my daily journal, read the national and business news in the morning papers, eat a good breakfast, get washed and dressed, and beat the morning rush hour by 15 minutes! Ha! I have seized the day, and life is good.

Upon my arrival at work, I am promptly informed by one of my contemporaries that Joe the Boss, my immediate supervisor, needs to see me and several others at a 10:00 A.M. meeting. SWOOSH! There goes my pondered, planned, productive day right down the toilet.

I show up at the conference room 5 minutes early, as usual, and proceed to sit idly by as half a dozen others show up late. Following the usual morning banter, the heart of the meeting gets underway at about 10:20 A.M., if I'm lucky.

The meeting is interrupted twice by phone calls to Joe. I twiddle my thumbs as Joe indicates to everyone whose time he considers least important.

The meeting takes about an hour, packed full of about 10 minutes worth of information. As I try to leave, Joe pulls me aside for a 5-minute, one-on-one exchange of information and ideas. Although Joe may not understand or accept the failure of the meeting that just took place, at least he is smart and successful enough to know the importance of one-on-one interaction.

The time is now 11:25 A.M. I have a lunch date planned—to discuss business. And when I return, I ignore all common sense and call a meeting with those people I directly supervise. After all, Joe needs to know that I found his information and direction important enough to occupy an hour's worth of my people's time. In a moment of weakness, an afternoon meeting seems, well, the right thing—the human thing—to do.

That evening, I leave work, wondering once again how the day I thought I had seized got away from me. Often, I take home the work I had hoped to accomplish at the office.

Besides the way they eat up my time, business meetings seem wrong for so many other reasons. Frequently, the most assertive people in the conference room veer the meeting off its agenda. Others play silly games of one-upmanship, hoping to gain favor with the boss. Many people—if not most—sit there quietly, listening to bad ideas being tossed around and hoping the spectacle soon will end. Sometimes these theatrics get in the way of the boss's message, muddling the information he had hoped to relate.

Lack of time. Lack of direction. Bad decision making. All because of business meetings.

Sound familiar? It should. Statistics indicate that managers spend about half of their workday in business meetings. For senior managers, the amount approaches three-quarters of their day. The time consumed, the politics, the tendency towards bad decision making—it's all a part of life, right?

Indeed, most managers surrender to meetings without realizing they're doing so. Holding meetings, at some point, becomes as natural as breathing. And the suggestion that these daily sessions are unproductive or bad for business doesn't register because there simply doesn't seem to be an alternative way of doing things.

Allow me to offer this alternative way, a different approach to managing—without meetings! Over the years, I have researched and, in some cases, worked with leaders who essentially have purged standard workplace meetings from their management regimen. I have successfully used many of their ideas to avoid calling together my team or coworkers. In fact, I can count the number of meetings I have convened over the last 10 years on one hand—not bad for someone who has a diverse background managing systems, projects, and groups of people from 7 to 70 strong. The results? A more creative and productive workday. A strong sense of personal direction and time efficiency. And, surprisingly, greater control over my team and the coworkers I depend on.

The first step to managing without meetings is to accept your distaste for them. This recognition may be more difficult than you think. After all, what could be more basic—more human—than wanting to bring together on a daily basis the people you are responsible for or rely upon? Having these workers in front of you certainly has the feel of hands-on control. If you have important information to distribute, it seems to make sense to pass it out, all at once, from mouth to ears. And if you are surrounded with competent people in a conference room, it seems appropriate to seek advice and information firsthand. On the surface, it all makes perfect sense. It's easy to see why you perhaps have allowed meetings to dominate your day.

And if you are called to a meeting, what could be more basic—more human—than wanting to attend? It could mean gaining some type of useful information. It could mean receiving work direction. And you could be asked to offer important advice to your boss or your coworkers. You would think that people would enthusiastically scramble for a meeting whenever one was called!

And yet, you know this eagerness is not the case. Like most people, you probably dread meetings. Underneath the rudimentary assumptions made about the benefits of holding a meeting, you sense, deep down, the uselessness—and the hindering effects—of these daily discussions.

Accept this underlying disgust with meetings. And then delve into the reasons for your repugnance.

EXPLORE YOUR DISTASTE FOR MEETINGS

So what is it with this inner loathing of meetings? Why do people generally groan when a meeting is called? Why are meetings hated by the people who schedule them, who conduct them, and who attend them?

The answers are there, once you are cognizant of meeting misgivings.

First, meetings take time—lots and lots of it. The time consumed is rarely well scheduled or well managed. Management studies suggest that about half of all time spent in a meeting is unproductive—and I would label those studies as generous. When you are at a meeting, even one that you have convened, your most valuable resource—time—is being used up.

I remember eating brown-bagged lunches during meetings back when I was a production manager. My boss had mandated my presence at daily machine status meetings, and I had figured that overlapping my lunch with this new requirement made for an efficient schedule. Looking back, it seems naïve, but I actually believed people would be impressed with my time maximization. Once, I showed up without the bag. "Well, Scott," my boss suggested dryly, "since you don't have your lunch, I assume you plan to join us today both in body *and* mind." Oops! No bag lunches after that comment.

I suppose attempting any other task during a meeting, even eating, is a bit impolite. However, the discourtesy isn't the problem. When a meeting is called, people are expected to give up not just their attention, but every aspect of their time. Part of the illusion at any workplace meeting is that everyone must at least seem interested.

When a meeting is in progress, *nothing* else involving the people on hand is taking place. No sales rep ever closed a big deal in the middle of a sales meeting. No construction worker ever poured a foundation during the site manager's morning meeting. No good plan or idea ever was carried out or monitored during a staff meeting. When meetings happen, nothing else does.

Many corporations spend large amounts of money to train their workers on management and time allocation skills. A company I worked for spent 2500 dollars for me to attend a two-day seminar on time management. Yes, I found the course interesting and insightful, but the corporate expense gave me pause, as I considered the aggregate cost to companies that sent thousands of people to such courses each year. Teaching workers to allocate their time and prioritize their tasks undoubtedly produces some sort of return on investment. But I doubt if even the best time allocator in the world can uncover the hour-and-a-half of productive time gained by canceling just one useless meeting.

Tracey Richards is a quality assurance engineer who discontinued her team's biweekly meetings in favor of individually visiting 10 auditors. "It's amazing how much more time efficient and productive it is to get with these auditors one at a time," she says.

The second reason we tend to hate meetings has to do with why most of us are asked to be a part of them. We're key players. Meetings often involve the people whose opinions and actions make things happen. Again, what could be more natural than for managers to want their movers and shakers in front of them each day, passing out firsthand information and guidance, and receiving firsthand feedback? But the same characteristics that make us an integral part of an organization also make us downright allergic to sitting in a meeting. Key people usually have a clear vision as to what needs to get done and how to make it so. We are decisive, opinionated, and full of ideas. So who wants to join a group of equally decisive, opinionated, and idea-filled people? Inevitably, our own voiced proposals are going to get watered down in this sea of stubbornness.

Have you ever sat through a meeting where you *knew* the person sitting next to you had the correct answer—and yet remained silent? In all likelihood, this person figured it was easier to count the minutes while others butted heads and then catch the boss later with undiluted recommendations. Who can blame anyone for using such a tactic?

Says quality assurance engineer Tracey Richards: "Nobody with the right idea wants to take the floor during a meeting. The best solution always comes out afterward. In a teleconference, my team secretly calls this good idea the 'call after the call.'"

Who can blame anyone that counts the minutes until the hodgepodge of thoughts, complaints, recommendations, and idle chatter is complete? When finished, the key people—the doers—can go back to their domains, their safe havens of responsibility where things can be considered with a laser beam of focus (until, of course, the next meeting comes along).

The third reason we hate meetings is that we have all grown weary of the games people play during them. People tend not to be themselves in the conference room. They become obnoxious to get attention, they lie if the truth does not fit, and they go along with whatever the crowd is doing. Chances are that the most juvenile displays you ever have seen at work took place in a meeting. Sadly, there is an inclination—a very human one—to join in one's surroundings. Therefore, you might have a problem pointing the finger and, in truth, you may play these games as well as anyone. (I know I'm guilty.)

Finally, we tend to hate meetings because nothing gets accomplished. Meetings hold a foul-smelling air of worthlessness that seems awkward to acknowledge. But why not just say it out loud? *Meetings are worthless!* It almost feels embarrassing to say, considering how many of your waking hours you spend in conference rooms. Who feels comfortable admitting that a huge chunk of life has been spent on something of no value? But getting past the discomfort is imperative.

In a moment of revelation, imagine yourself ripping off your clothing, standing on the biggest rock of the highest hilltop, and shouting, "Meetings are worthless!"

"But why?" an imaginary passerby may ask, as you are shouting this assertion, naked on top of a rock.

Let's consider why.

RECOGNIZE THE WORTHLESSNESS OF MEETINGS

Years ago, I had the pleasure of hearing the notorious former U.S. Secretary of State Alexander Haig give a speech, only a few weeks before declaring himself a candidate for president of the United States.

Haig began with a funny story about Ronald Reagan, in whose administration he had served. He referred to a report—without actually confirming it—hinting that Reagan used to nod off during full Cabinet meetings. "Sometimes, when I approached the president with an idea, he said he'd have to sleep on it," said Haig with a smile. "I was always confident the process would begin immediately!"

The story paints an interesting picture. Assuming there is an element of truth to it, one has to wonder about the president of the United States dozing off during Cabinet meetings. Granted, Reagan was in his 70s. But is this not the man whose election campaigns and management style remain topics in today's political discussions? Is this not the man who comfortably could make a key decision—and stand behind it for years—based on the facts he read off an index card? Regardless of the politics, Reagan remains a study in fast-paced leadership. So what was this man doing sleeping in a conference room packed with members of his administration? Perhaps Reagan, in his wisdom, recognized the worthlessness of these meetings and simply decided to use the time more wisely.

John Frost has headed various manufacturing and process improvement projects for General Electric and Johnson & Johnson, sometimes managing facilities with as many as 600 workers. He is currently head of process improvement for Johnson & Johnson's disposable contact lens division in Jacksonville, Florida. In spite of managing large groups of people and experiencing the temptation to convene big staffs, Frost accepted the futility of meetings years ago. Says one former member of Frost's team: "In the year and a half I worked with John, he never once called a meeting!"

Frost believes in the customer-service approach to his employees. That is, he treats each team member as a customer and believes that keeping a team member in a meeting is akin to keeping a customer waiting in a store. "I'm not adding value to the customer relationship by keeping a team member bogged down in a meeting," he suggests. He says that a personal connection between a boss and a worker begins the moment the worker is set free to go and carry out great deeds.

How can you recognize the worthlessness of the meetings *you* convene or attend? You can start by asking a few, basic questions:

Is useful information actually getting through to the people who are attending?

Perhaps you call meetings because you like the idea that information gets passed on to everyone at the same time. Seems understandable. But are you getting through? Are the 10 nodding heads in front of you *really* digesting the data, guidance, and work direction you're handing out?

Try this experiment the next time you hold a conference. Put out an item you consider important. Make it something slightly more complicated than a *yes or no* decision. Ideally, you should read it from a piece of paper, as if it were just handed to you. Then, the following day, separately tell a few people who attended the meeting that you lost the paper and were wondering if they had the information on hand. You may be amazed to find how few of them can repeat it back to you or have it available in written notes.

I had a boss who once announced at a morning meeting, with all staff members present, that the company was treating everyone to lunch that day because our plant had reduced quality-rejected production by more than one percent over the last year. (We were one of only three locations nationwide that had exceeded this corporate goal.) He congratulated everyone and made it quite clear how much this achievement meant to him and to the plant's reputation.

Later that day, as the caterers arrived, he asked me, "Do you think anyone has any idea why we're feeding them?"

I hesitated, sensing a loaded question, and then responded. "Yes, I believe you made it quite clear at your meeting how important their achievement was. I think they know."

"Hmmm. Let's find out."

It was a bad call on my part. As my boss and I wandered the plant, he asked most of the people who had been in the conference room what the free lunch was all about. I will give them credit: virtually everyone ventured a guess. But after asking a dozen people, not one had offered the correct answer. (How had *I* known when he had asked me earlier? I would like to think it had been my great listening skills, but it probably had been a fluke.) My boss—realizing how few people had been paying attention that morning—looked like an abandoned puppy.

Here's a thought. Had he walked around earlier that day, in lieu of holding a meeting, shaking hands with his staff and congratulating them one-on-one, would more people have known the correct answer to his question later in the day?

Some managers have it figured out. John Decker is a packaging and shipping supervisor for Bethlehem Steel. He manages about 50 people and, over the last 10 years, has cut back dramatically on the number of meetings he uses to lead them. "When I took over the team, there was something called a weekly communications meeting that used to last five hours," he says. "Considering the amount of information that was actually getting through to people, it was an easy thing to do away with."

How many people leave a meeting knowing the important point or two that was covered? Decker puts the ratio at one-third. "If you have 10 people in a room," he contends, "only 3 or 4 will walk away knowing and understanding what has been discussed."

Are the people in attendance actually providing useful information and advice?

If meetings often fail in disseminating information downward, then how well do they work in communicating ideas upward?

Do you hold meetings to gather data and advice? Does it seem to work? If not, don't take it personally. Due to human quirks, information acquired from people during standard organizational meetings is often filtered, distorted, incomplete, or inaccurate.

Remember the person who was sitting next to you, the one you *knew* had the right answer but chose to sit quietly? Remember something you learned at a meeting that turned out to be erroneous?

When you base your managerial decisions on information and advice garnered solely at a meeting, you may be doing your team and yourself a disservice.

Are these meetings solving any problems? Are the solutions any better than the problems?

Perhaps you like to call people into a conference room for a daily or weekly "meeting of the minds," where the great thinkers in your organization can join together to solve common problems.

You might realize by now that these problems often do not get properly addressed. Sometimes they don't even get brought up. Why? Meetings invariably get off track because they become whirlwinds of immediate crises ("fires" that need putting out) and priorities handed down from above. Many times, meetings cave in to ulterior motives, personal agendas, and grandstanding.

But what about those times when important, long-term problems *do* get brought up? You would think that placing a group of experts in a room would produce reliable solutions. Unfortunately, corporate, political, and military history tells us differently. Such chronicles are filled with stories of great leaders—in meeting settings—conceiving and embracing bad initiatives.

Great minds can and often do join together in dynamic and ingenious ways to find solutions. However, I suggest that these minds are brought together by creative management and by effective one-on-one exchanges of ideas, and not by the failed structure of a staff meeting. The key is to gather knowledge and recommendations from others necessary to make important decisions, without the flawed group dynamics that occur when people are physically brought together.

ACCEPT THE FLAWED NATURE OF PEOPLE

You might ask, "Can't meetings be more useful if people just learn to run them better?"

Indeed, many managers have sought ways to improve their methods for holding meetings, hoping to make these get-togethers more productive and free of bad ideas. Many books have been written on how to run meetings better, and most of them are quite good. I give credit to those people—business, academic, and otherwise—who study the nature of meetings in an attempt to improve them. However, I respectfully suggest that they miss the point: holding a meeting creates problems that are unfixable because the structure of a meeting is inherently defective.

In other words, you can't fix something that was never working to begin with. Human nature dictates that when three or more people are in a room at once—whether they are a work team, an assembly line crew, a corporate committee, a general's staff, or a presidential cabinet—the decisions they come up with are often and predictably flawed.

There's a name for the concept. It's called *groupthink*—the tendency of individuals in a group gathering, in the name of conformity, to sit back quietly and allow a bad idea to develop a life of its own. Once the idea takes form, the group often buys into it completely.

U.S. military officers are taught about groupthink with the hope they might avoid becoming prey to it. Tactical instructors teach how, throughout history, intelligent, surefooted strategy planners got together as a group and failed miserably in formulating feasible combat operations. The prominent military example is John F. Kennedy's decision in early 1961 to help 1500 Cuban exiles launch an attack at the Bay of Pigs, with the outrageous notion that this small incursion would somehow rally the people of Cuba to overthrow Fidel Castro! After training them, the U.S. helped the exiles mount the attack, only to pull out its own air support at the last minute, leaving them to certain death or imprisonment. In later years, several attendees of the Kennedy planning sessions openly discussed the decision-making process (perhaps out of hopeful justification, or perhaps out of a cleansing penance). The one thing they all agreed on was how *right* the decision seemed at the time—as a group, in those meetings.

The obvious political example of groupthink is the series of decisions in the early 1970s, by Richard Nixon and his tight group of advisors, to go after people on an enemies list and to cover up their direct or indirect involvement in the break-in of the Democratic National Committee Headquarters at the Watergate Hotel. Historians and psychologists had a unique chance—because of taped, high-level meetings eventually released to the public—to analyze the way grown men, as a group, could conjure up such childlike paranoia and create such diabolical plans. Looking back, the misdeeds of a president and his staff all those years ago still make us pause and reflect. But for hundreds of years to come, the truly scandalous aspect of the entire Watergate affair will be the decision-making process, in meetings, that led up to it.

What about the *corporate* world? Are business people so naturally pliable during group decision making? Maybe, maybe not. But one thing is for certain: behind any well-known business failing in recent history—huge corporations buckling under questionable accounting practices, giant investment firms throwing their good names behind profitless dot-coms, large management companies building endless office space and seeing it sit barren—there were documented business meetings. At these meetings, otherwise talented, insightful, and charismatic people sat quietly rather than voice their concerns or objections.

How, for instance, could successful, proven business people—the best of the best—get together and decide, as a group, to change the taste of the most popular soft drink in America? In 1985, it happened, and it was a disaster.

"People become too polite as members of a team," suggests corporate recruiter Dan Bessinger. "There's too much effort to accommodate all ideas until a dozen potentially good ideas are blended together into one really bad one." He should know: he fought groupthink as a manufacturing general manager for 20 years.

It boggles the mind—but it shouldn't. Group dynamics, in many ways, is an exact science.

Experts on group dynamics suggest that the easiest way to counteract groupthink is to designate someone at every meeting as a devil's advocate. Experts recommend that at any meeting where decisions are being made, someone should be in charge of picking apart every suggestion, with the hope of chopping down a bad idea before it takes root.

Hey, now *there's* a job for everyone to fight over! In real-world application, can you imagine successfully scrutinizing the ideas of everyone else in the conference room? Even if it were expected of you, would you want to start picking apart the *boss's* ideas, no matter how obviously flawed? My personal experience is that a devil's advocate's success is thwarted by the very thing that makes such a role necessary—the lack of ability to exercise individuality and clear thought in a group.

Another human characteristic that makes the meeting an intrinsically flawed vehicle is the older, more easily understood concept we know as peer pressure. All it takes is a stroll through any corporate parking lot to figure out that peer pressure does not end with acne medication. We all desire the toys of the boy or girl next door. With all the hoopla about a diversified society, I would argue that, with improved communications worldwide, humans are more preoccupied with conformity than ever. Is it possible to walk through a work lounge or break room without hearing people discuss how fast their cars are, how well their stocks are is doing, or how much RAM their computers have?

Whether you want to accept it or not, the reality is that you have a very strong, innate need to be accepted and to conform to what others expect you to be. One of the great founders of humanistic psychology, Abraham Maslow, argued that, after water, food, sex, and security, there is no greater need for humans than the desire for affirmation by others. It is greater than the need for self-respect, prestige, personal success, and self-fulfillment.

Rather than hopelessly surrender to—or, worse still, fight against—these human tendencies, why not accept them as part of what we are as people? When facing nature, your best bet is to work around it.

STOP CALLING MEETINGS FOR THE WRONG (REAL) REASONS

Suppose that you asked a group of managers to explain why they convene meetings. They might respond by jotting down a list of reasons, and their list might look like this one:

- We hold meetings because we believe they are appropriate tools for passing out information and work direction, for voicing concerns, and exchanging ideas.
- We hold meetings to get people on the same sheet of music.
- We hold meetings because we like having workers present. It gives us a feeling of control and a sense that advice and information from competent people are immediately available.

- We hold meetings to bring good minds together to solve problems.

- We hold meetings so that individual department heads can report on a daily basis.

- We hold meetings for workers to get together and bridge their differences.

- We hold meetings to create mutually agreed upon work parameters and quality controls.

Now consider your faint sense of dread and distaste for meetings and the perception of worthlessness it alludes to. Do any of those splendid things just listed *really* happen at meetings? Do information and work direction actually get across to people? Do ideas get properly passed around? Are problems solved by competent minds? Have you ever sat through a meeting that, in fact, resulted in a commonsense list of goals or policies?

If you think hard enough, you might be able to recollect a productive meeting or two. Then again, maybe not. The successful business meeting is not so much a myth as it is a holy grail: you may believe it exists, and you may be on a crusade to find it—but you have never seen it yourself.

Such pondering leads us to a crucial question. If managers, deep down, hate meetings, and if they sense that meetings are useless, then why do they, as a global corporate society, tolerate them? Why isn't there an international uprising against them? Why do we endure a vehicle for disseminating and deliberating information that produces little more than bad decisions and wasted business time?

The ugly answer is that many managers, whether they realize it or not, often hold meetings for a list of reasons considerably different from the one just mentioned.

I offer to you the following as a *reality list*:

- Managers tend to hold meetings because that's what their peers are doing.

- Managers hold meetings because of corporate mandates requiring that certain types of meetings be convened. In other words, they hold meetings because they are told to.

- Managers hold meetings because they perceive personal short-comings in how they utilize other management techniques, such as one-on-one managing, employing transformational leadership, and delegating.

- Sometimes they hold meetings because it allows them to avoid other, more meaningful and productive undertakings.

- Managers hold meetings to give themselves a false sense that something has been accomplished.

I contend that in spite of their own bad experiences in the conference room, most managers just can't stop convening meetings themselves. It reminds me of the question you occasionally may ask yourself as a parent: "Why do I find myself saying the same awful things to my children that my parents said to me—and that I swore back then I'd never say to *my* kids?" When people pass from childhood to parenthood, they do, indeed, find themselves making the same parental decisions and mistakes. After all, their perspective is now different, and their decision-making processes are clouded by the overwhelming responsibilities that parenting brings. The same can be said about managing at your place of work. When you are merely an attendee at a meeting, you sit there and squirm—bored, helpless, and upset over the fruitlessness of what is taking place. However, when you move one more step up the corporate ladder, your perspective changes. All the boredom, helplessness, and resentment are mentally blocked out. *You* are in charge now— you *must* hold meetings.

Look into yourself and examine your own reasons for disliking meetings but then holding them anyway. It is the important first step that will help you stop surrendering to them.

SUMMARY

- The goals of a business meeting are rarely met.
- Deep down, most managers not only hate meetings but also understand their uselessness.
- Meetings cannot be fixed. Due to human nature, they are inherently flawed.
- Managers often hold meetings for the wrong reasons, including their perceived inability to run things any differently.
- The first step to managing without meetings is to accept and explore your distaste for them and stop surrendering to them.

CHAPTER 2

Recognize What Doesn't Work and Why

KNOW YOUR ENEMY

After you decide to stop surrendering to meetings, your next step is to understand just what elements comprise a meeting and what makes it doomed to fail. If successful leadership and time effectiveness are your goals, then the standard workplace meeting is your enemy. Know your enemy as you prepare your strategy for defeating it.

On the surface, it seems somewhat absurd describing what a meeting is. It's like Potter Stewart, as an associate justice on the Supreme Court, explaining back in 1964 how to identify pornography. "I know it when I see it," he proclaimed.

However, if you're not fully aware of the ominous signs of a meeting that's a-brewin', you might wind up like the frog in the pot of water who didn't know the water was warming to a boil until it was too late.

The enemy has five main characteristics, or components.

Three or more people

A meeting requires three or more people communicating at the same time—presumably at somewhere other than the water cooler. It can consist of as few as three people in an office or as many as an auditorium packed with enraged workers. Two people do not constitute a meeting. To the contrary, my experience is that one-on-one communication is so effective that it is better to contact 10 people individually for six minutes at a time than to meet with 10 people for an hour. When three or more individuals combine, the flawed nature of people takes over, time is wasted, and bad ideas are conceived.

A moderator

Meetings don't just happen. They need to be convened. Since people intuitively hate meetings and understand their uselessness, there probably wouldn't be too many of them if managers didn't seek to create them and run them. Sometimes moderators are reluctant hosts if they have been directed by others to hold certain types of meetings. But more often, the moderator is the meeting's creator—fooling himself into thinking something is going to get accomplished.

The sharing of real time

From a time management perspective, the sharing of real time is the worst aspect of a meeting. In order for people to have their time occupied simultaneously, they must clear huge swathes of their appointment schedules—whereas the simple sharing of information (rather than time) might have been handled individually in smaller, more efficient doses (using e-mails, one-on-one discussions, etc.).

When people are kept under enemy control at the same time, time inefficiency gives way to time surrendering.

A loose agenda and goals

A cluster of people usually doesn't take on the ugly form of a meeting until a loose agenda makes itself known. At staff meetings, the agenda might be routine and carried out in habitlike fashion. Other times, the agenda might be announced just prior to things getting started.

While a meeting's loose agenda is often understood, its objectives are not always straightforward. In fact, they're often murky to everyone but the moderator. Perhaps it's better this way. Since the goals of a meeting are rarely met, the fewer people who know about them the better. If you sense that there are goals to a particular get-together—even if you don't know what they are—there's a good chance the enemy is at hand.

The gathering of information

Meetings are held with the hope of garnering useful information. When you see the moderator's attention go around the conference table, soliciting data and opinions from different people representing different departments, there's a strong probability a meeting is going on—and just as strong a likelihood that some of the information is inaccurate, downplayed, or exaggerated. For reasons already stated, much of the data gathered at a meeting is suspect.

Unquestionably, these factors have some of their own, individual merit. No one begrudges a manager for bringing people together, taking charge, sharing time, formulating an agenda and goals, or attempting to collect pertinent information. However, when these elements are combined, they tend to work against one another, deteriorating into the dark swill that is the useless meeting. Watch for these components as you hone your meeting radar.

IDENTIFY YOUR ENEMY'S SOLDIERS

Know the foot soldiers that serve your enemy. When it comes to wasting your time, each of these warriors has a special talent. You are likely to find at least one of them at every meeting you attend.

Here are the 10 conference room combatants along with their distinguishing features.

Armageddon Al

Armageddon Al is easy to spot. He's the one warning everybody that the world is coming to an end.

It doesn't take much to make Al think his world is crumbling. It could be an announced change in procedure, a new task, a visit from a regional manager, a group criticism, a company financial statement, a news article—anything! You would think that, like the boy who cried *wolf*, Al eventually would be ignored. But people in a meeting are continuously drawn to Al and his game. He gets lots of attention.

Backstabbing Bill

Make sure you attend every meeting you're ever invited to, if you don't want your name brought up by Backstabbing Bill. Sometimes it doesn't matter, though. Bill can stick it to you just as well while you're sitting there. He's got it down to a fine art. For example, he might say something to the boss that's holding the meeting like, "Well, the project would have gotten done sooner had I gotten the people I requested." Needless to say, *you're* the one he had asked for those people. There may have been several perfectly good reasons for not giving up the people Bill needed (including the fact that he already had wormed his way into having too many workers transferred from your department). But never mind. Now you're in a defensive posture at the meeting, which was all Bill really wanted.

Blaming others or attracting attention to others keeps attention away from his own incompetence. That's the way Bill likes to do battle.

Blind Bob

There's a very easy way to solve all problems: deny they exist! In Bob's world, people never make mistakes, machinery never needs fixing, and pertinent issues never need addressing.

"Bob, we ran out of raw materials again for our Saturday production crew. What's wrong with our weekend supply forecasting?"

"There's *nothing* wrong with it."

"Bob, the machine drive motor is speeding up and slowing down erratically. What's wrong with the speed control?"

"There's *nothing* wrong with it."

"Bob, I saw three people in the last 10 minutes without their cut-resistant gloves on. What's wrong with our protective gear policy?"

"There's *nothing* wrong with it."

"Oh. Thanks, Bob. Sorry to have bothered you."

Here is someone willing to argue for an hour that a problem doesn't exist, rather than take 10 proactive minutes to fix it.

Bob is especially dangerous at meetings, where blindness is contagious. What easier way to move onto the next topic than to have everyone lulled into the notion that the current topic need not be considered? If groupthink is the fire that reduces good solutions to ashes, then Bob is surely the fuel that keeps it burning.

What's causes Bob's blindness? Is it pure, unadulterated optimism? Is it laziness? Misinformation? Perhaps it's just ignorance, sweet ignorance. They say it's bliss—and Blind Bob is one happy son of a gun.

Devious Drew

If Blind Bob isn't denying a problem, then Devious Drew is swaying your attention away from it.

Here's the scenario:

The morning staff meeting is about to start. Everyone is waiting for Drew to arrive, as he has some explaining to do. Several organizational shortcomings point directly to his department.

So, in walks Drew, who loudly proclaims, "Gee, I just walked past the railroad dock. Not one railcar is blue-flagged or chocked. What the hell is going on around here?" This is a serious company safety infraction, the type that gets people fired. Therefore, a major portion of the staff meeting is spent assigning blame and future responsibility. An informal investigation is started. Company safety policy is reviewed and emphasized. Everyone leaves the meeting understanding the new priority of the minute.

Devious Drew is not just a pompous loudmouth. He is also a master sleight-of-hand artist, misdirecting attention away from the hand with the hidden ball.

Jovial Janet

Hey, she's the life of the party! Always the first to arrive and the last to leave, Janet's friendly, witty, and full of office gossip. She brings doughnuts and pours coffee, perking everyone's spirits.

Janet will talk endlessly about everything. Unless someone pulls the meeting back to the subject at hand, she'll continue on her own agenda for its entirety. And unless the subject at hand involves who's dating whom, who's on the way up or who's on the way down, consider Janet out of the conversation. She doesn't care about the day-to-day things that make the organization work, and her indifference has led to a mild case of incompetence.

Lapdog Lawrence

Lawrence's quirk is his unfailing adoration for management. Similar to Blind Bob, Lawrence is quick to deny problems exist, not because he's blind to them, but because *nothing* could possibly be going wrong in *his* boss's domain.

And if something *is* going wrong, then obviously the *boss's* solution is the best. If the boss is concerned, then so's Lawrence. If the boss tells a bad joke, Lawrence laughs. Oblivious loyalty is Lawrence's game. Everyone knows it and everyone condemns it, but he still helps managers to render meetings useless.

Pious Pete

Pete is the most holy of employees. He is quick to quote office rules off the top of his head. Be careful not to ignore him, or you might find the stone tablets of corporate policy crashing down upon you.

Like most saints, Pete sits comfortably on a cloud—the foggy cloud of regulation, that is. Whether or not the written method has anything to do with common sense is irrelevant. Modifying the regulation is out of the question. He sits there in the conference room, his look of scorn aimed at anyone who would consider trying something a different, better way.

A quick study of Pete reveals the true nature of his godliness. As with most humans, Pete is a creature of habit and a hater of change. Further examination shows yet another ulterior motive: Pete is a little lazy. Change and positive action require far more effort than memorizing and enforcing petty regulations.

Shoot-it-down Susie

An exceptional employee, Susie also serves as the true devil's advocate—to the death! Quick to rebuke any idea or tear apart the details of its execution, Susie carries the role of skeptical scrutinizer to the extreme. Yes, an uncompassionate critic is good to have around, and she often sways the numb masses away from the wrong path. But gee, Susie, give us a break! There are *some* good ideas out there.

Between Susie and the other soldiers, it's a wonder how any plan ever makes it from start to finish. As with most of these personalities, Susie knows one game best. In her case, it's criticism. Please don't ask her for her own ideas or solutions. Positive contribution is another game, and odds are she's not playing.

Silent Saul

Saul is a good man, a hard worker, and a conscientious employee. And he has never said a word, good or bad, at any meeting in his life. But don't be critical of his silence. Still waters run deep. Chances are he's interested in joining the other side and fighting the plethora of meetings he's asked to attend. But his continuing reticence ensures his place with the enemy.

Workhorse Willy

Every organization has a Willy. He is *the* model employee. He's hardworking and innovative, and his positive manner rubs off onto others. He's also very knowledgeable about the company and the ways it operates. If an extra difficult task needs finishing in a hurry, give it to Willy.

Willy is also good to have at meetings. He participates enthusiastically and is quick to offer recommendations when asked. During any meeting, when the boss hands him yet another project, he simply smiles, nods his head, and writes down what's expected of him onto his notepad. Willy is one hell of a great guy.

So what makes Willy an enemy soldier? It's the way he baffles everyone when, one day, he turns in his resignation and is gone in a flash! No explanation, no theatrics, no good-byes—just *poof!* and he's gone.

And boy, what a gap he leaves. Things start crumbling fast without Willy around, and playing catch-up is no fun, especially with the types of things he was able to handle. No need to worry, however. Another Willy will come along soon enough, and soon he, too, will have too much on his plate.

By taking on too much at meetings, Willy becomes his own worst enemy—and yours.

You would think that with such an array of characters, nothing would *ever* get decided on at meetings. It's funny how, because of group dynamics, they often *do* come together—to make bad decisions, that is.

Marketing expert and political strategist Erik Skaggs suggests that, rather than keeping these temperaments in check, most meeting hosts oblige them. "Managers who hold large meetings often find themselves serving the role of psychologist," he observes. "They spend much of their time trying to accommodate the various personality types and feelings that have invaded the room. The empty goal becomes trying to make everybody feel good about themselves."

Make sure you know who these characters—these soldiers—are. If you find yourself listening to one of them, there's a good chance the enemy—that is, a useless meeting—has taken over the room.

IDENTIFY CAMOUFLAGED TARGETS

Sometimes the standard workplace meeting can be disguised as something else. That doesn't make it any more useful, but it may catch you off guard as you try to cut back on the meetings you convene and attend.

Here are some of the best-camouflaged meetings.

The unscheduled meeting

This type of meeting is almost conventional in its ostensible unconventionality. Every organization has one of those bosses that frantically hunts down all team members, calls them into the office, and proceeds to hold a meeting on whatever *the* hot topic is that day. If not the entire staff, a few key players might be pulled aside to discuss a new issue.

There are good and bad aspects of the unscheduled meeting— mostly bad. On the good side, if a manager is holding mostly unscheduled meetings, then at least there's the implication he's trying to cut down on his *scheduled* meetings. On the bad side, all of the five elements of a meeting remain intact. In fact, the meeting trait of sharing real time is magnified when folks are pulled away from their work unexpectedly. At least when facing a scheduled meeting, people can attempt to plan some work around this black hole in their day. The unscheduled meeting shows up like a creature in the night, snatching them up and dragging them into an unproductive darkness.

Introducing the new boss

Let's say a new manager has just taken over a department in the company. The logical thing for her to do, it seems, is to get everyone together to introduce herself. She can tell of her background, and she can put out her *commander's intent*—her particular vision for the department. She can set priorities and perhaps even establish a timetable for needed changes. If the group seems receptive, she can answer questions. On the surface, the introduction meeting seems logical, even expected.

What is gained from meeting all your workers in an audience setting? Does it put everyone on the same sheet of music? Does it inform? Does it motivate? No. No. No. What does it do? It pulls people away from their jobs—as any other meeting does.

I suggest that the better way for this new manager to be effective is never to introduce herself to the department as a group. There is much to be gained as the new boss no one *really* knows. It allows her to spend her first few weeks observing, listening—without any preconceptions on the part of her department. She can meet people one-on-one, solicit input and opinions, without showing her hand of cards right at the start of the card game. I once watched the new manager of a paper mill introduce himself in such a manner over a month's time. He learned a lot about his people and his operation.

Suppose, at an introduction meeting, a new manager stated bluntly, "One of my missions is to put a cap on hiring and do more with less." If adding a few positions might actually help a flawed department, wouldn't everyone, after the meeting, be hesitant to explain why? Observing, listening, and understanding will make this new, good manager a new, great manager.

Think of the logistics and lost work time involved with gathering together an entire department. Suppose there are 100 people in this department. Assume the best case scenario: half an hour to assemble everyone, an hour to address the department, and half an hour to get everyone back to work. Two hours of lost work time.

Now, how long would it take, with everyone *still working*, to walk through the entire department, shaking hands, learning faces, asking questions, perhaps taking notes? In which scenario would people feel better about the person they just met?

Some years ago, I watched one of the most confusing television ad campaigns ever. In one TV spot, a new, real-life CEO formally introduces himself to his workers (and, I guess, to his customers via the spot). He recently has taken over a large but unsuccessful grocery chain, and he is bent on turning things around. During these 30-second commercials, he gives a rousing speech, promising to bring back lost customers. The camera pans the audience—presumably employees—

as they sit there smiling and nodding pensively. My wife said it best when she remarked: "What a crock! For years, we've stayed away from that grocery chain because the stores are disorganized and overpriced. If he *really* wanted to impress me, he'd be on that commercial listening to his workers and his customers, instead of putting on a show for a bunch of people pretending to be interested." The same could be said for any new manager that begins his assignment by lecturing his workers. What a crock.

The lunch meeting

There's nothing wrong with a manager ordering out lunch for a staff meeting. If people are receiving nourishment, at least *something* is getting accomplished.

Also, it's great when a manager takes out his key players for lunch every now and then. Food is the ultimate, immediate positive reinforcement for both a single job well done and ongoing good performance.

However, I submit that lunch with an agenda is unproductive. First, any way you decorate the sandwich, it's still a sandwich, and any way you decorate a meeting, it's still a meeting. Second, by the time we reach a certain age (I won't say what I think that age is) we all become passionate about food. (Perhaps it's because other passions are subsiding!) My experience is that trying to get thoughtful input from people intimately engaged in eating is futile. Finally, eating takes blood away from the brain to the digestive system. We just don't think as much or as sharply during and after a good meal. Do you *really* need input or ideas from food-happy fools rubbing their happy tummies?

The golf outing

As with the lunch get-together, there is nothing wrong with a manager taking out her staff for a golf outing, as long as there is no meeting agenda to the outing. As with food, many people are passionate about golf, and tapping into people's ideas or looking for a consensus while on the links is not likely to yield good results.

To be sure, there are many zealous golfers in the world of business. The sport is a mainstay of corporate culture and seems to serve two business purposes. First, it's utilized as a way of attracting clients and closing deals. Second, it's used by managers to gain information and consensus from their people—not to mention learning a thing or two about each person's self-discipline and composure.

I don't dispute the first intention. Many a great business deal has been sealed on a golf course. Celebrity golf coach Bruce Ollstein agrees. "When it comes to closing an important sales deal," he says, "there is nothing like taking your client out for 18 holes on a nice day."

However, the second notion—that of managing and consensus building while golfing—not only parallels the bad characteristics of a staff meeting but suggests a few more detrimental quirks as well.

A good friend of mine is the head of a quality control department for a major U.S. company. He recently told me of management colleagues stressing out during their golf lessons. "Why were they pressured?" I asked.

"Because," he stated matter-of-factly, "their careers are at stake."

Supercoach Ollstein understands the phenomenon. He has seen unfortunate power struggles on the golf course when the gamesmanship was high. "Sometimes artificial hierarchies are created by

3 8

the best golfers," he suggests. "If group decisions—about things that have nothing to do with golf—are being swayed by the person with the best swing, then certainly the best decisions aren't always being made."

The temptation to turn a golf outing into a camouflaged business meeting is apparent enough. Eighteen holes of golf mean at least four hours of real-time interaction between strong-minded, time-pressed people. The transition from team-building to competitive idea-crunching is seamless. It's no wonder that so many managers equate golf with business acumen.

I suggest that we're reaching a time in corporate history—perhaps due to the much-publicized successes of proudly unconventional managers—when some companies aren't as consumed with managers "punching tickets" or molding themselves into clichés, including the cliché about the boss putting in his office. If for no other reason, avoiding the golf outing as a team meeting allows you to fully tap into the resources of both your golfing and nongolfing cadre.

KNOW WHAT IS NOT A TARGET

There are some gatherings that seem like meetings and possess one or more of the five meeting traits—but are not meetings and, therefore, not the enemy.

Be realistic. There are times when getting people together is not only important but essential to maintaining any flourishing organization. None of the following types of congregation get in the way of the meetingless manager. They are fundamental to good management, and they all work.

Training

Few things in life are scarier than being thrown headfirst into a task without knowing anything about it. Lamentably, it seems like that's how most of us began our jobs. How sad, considering that a modest amount of work training could have made all the difference in the world. People feel more comfortable with their employer and their new positions if formal training programs exist. Ideally, the classroom material is minimal and hands-on training makes up the core curriculum.

Talk-through, walk-through rehearsals

If your organization has a major undertaking coming up, or if there's a project where several departments have to come together at once (an example might be a large-scale security team planning for the arrival of a guarded celebrity), then what better way is there to prepare for the task than to conduct a rehearsal?

Here's how it works. First, everybody is physically brought together, so that not only do they understand their own responsibilities, but they also understand what others will be doing at the same time. Each department (possibly each person) reviews their specific obligations during this mission. The moderator fields questions—even the dumbest of the dumb (yes, Virginia, there *is* such a thing as a dumb question)—in order for the most people possible to leave the room knowing what's expected. (Not *everyone* will know, as mentioned in Chapter 1.)

Then people are sent to their workplaces. The leader proceeds to these various locations, asking detailed, pertinent questions about individual roles and responsibilities. People are asked how they will respond if certain things go wrong. The leader repeats the process if necessary.

When a complex procedure involves many people doing the right thing at once, nothing beats the talk-through, walk-through rehearsal.

Customer reviews

If your business has a big customer that can make or break your business, it makes good professional sense to have this customer visit periodically. Along with a tour, the visit should include a conference with the customer and all of your key players, especially those that are able to address the customer's specific concerns.

Sometimes the customer plays host. I have attended quarterly "vendor reviews," where a few people from my company visited our customer's location and met with a room full of its key players.

In either case, the desire to satisfy the customer tends to bore a hole through the baggage that comes along with most standard meetings. Unless these get-togethers happen too often, they tend to be useful and necessary.

Seminars

Next to pay raises and time off, the preeminent sign of appreciation for good performance is to show interest in someone's personal development as a member of your organization. Why not show to an up-and-comer you're interested by sending that person to a seminar? Many organizations have a detailed schedule of seminars that they either conduct or sponsor in-house. Often, an instructor can come directly to your place of business. These sessions usually run from three days to three weeks and cover an array of topics, from specifically tailored technical knowledge to generic information about good work or management habits. Be careful to weed out the seminars that have been attended by your workers and have received poor reviews.

If you are able to send a certain number of people each year away to seminars, please don't allow these slots to be taken over by your organization's deadwood. Yes, it's always painful to free up your good people to attend such things: sending away the do-nothings is easier, plus it gets rid of your troubles for a while. But it will build resentment in the long run. Therefore, choose the harder right over the easier wrong. Give up the people you'd rather not do without, and consider it a good, long-term investment in your organization. They won't be gone forever, and you and your team will benefit later on.

Conferences and conventions

Sending good people away to conventions, especially technical or trade conventions, is similar to sending them off to seminars. Both conventions and seminars bring together people of similar backgrounds. The twist on conventions is that, by design, they bring together people from different organizations. Many successful people are secretive about their success—until they're faced with a group of colleagues they've never met before. Once they're among new friends in their field, they tend to enjoy sharing their accomplishments—and the methods behind them. Conventions are where you find these people and take advantage of their helpful, interesting stories. Instead of asking folks in your organization to reinvent the wheel, why not send a few of them to a convention, where they can learn everything there is to know *about* wheels! Who knows—if one or two of them has a success story, perhaps they can contribute to the agenda (the ultimate ego booster).

Shift changes

If your job involves shift work, it's important for each position to be properly "relieved." An adequate amount of time should exist for one-on-one exchanges of information. The arriving worker should understand what's important and what's going wrong before the outgoing worker leaves. These position briefings should be monitored randomly by a manager.

As you might imagine, I argue against all of the arriving workers getting together during the start of the shift, for reasons already mentioned. Add one more reason: it takes responsibility for a good shift change briefing away from the individual.

Group complimenting

Complimenting a group (or an individual, for that matter) is not something we should take lightly as managers. A proper compliment takes practice. It involves good listening skills, with the manager learning how the performance happened so that it can be encouraged again. It includes a good word, perhaps an appropriate reward. A proper compliment stands on its own, not intermingled with criticism or other business.

Pep talks and breathers

My first job as a manager in the corporate world had one small draw-back: I hadn't the slightest clue what was going on.

My company had been interested primarily in my education and military background and was willing to overlook my nonexistent manufacturing experience. The plant's machinery, its production processes, and the manner in which things got accomplished were wondrous and exotic. Were it not for the yellow-painted walkways, I wouldn't have known even where to step!

One evening, after I had been assigned to my new production team, the machine plugged up so badly, we were looking at hours of cleaning up. It was pure muscle work, around dark, hard-to-get-at spots and steam pipes. I did what was expected of me: I panicked—and then I called Dave, my boss and mentor.

When Dave arrived, he jumped in to help, and we all sweated for half an hour. Having been trained to prevent heat exhaustion, I suggested we start rotating folks to the break room. "I've got a better idea," he said, and did something that caught me completely off guard. He told everyone to stop working. "Who wants a soda?" he asked. The entire team made its way to the break room and sucked in the air condi-tioning while Dave broke into a story about how finicky this old machine had been over the years. About half an hour later, he stood up. "Now listen," he said paternally. "I know this is about as bad as it gets around here. But we'll get through this—we always have. Let's just take it slow and safe and help each other out."

From an immediate time-efficiency standpoint, my suggestion of rotating the workers had made the most sense. But after all was said and done—and the machine was humming again about an hour earlier than I had expected—I believe Dave's breather and pep talk was probably the most well-invested 30 minutes I've ever witnessed.

A final thought on detecting the symptoms of a meeting. It often has been said that the smartest thing the Devil ever did was to convince people he didn't exist. The same can be said for defenders of the workplace meeting. Meeting partisans have somehow lulled us all into complacency with meetings, at times quietly convincing us that we aren't even at a meeting and that our time is not being wasted. Remember that the enemy is out there. It is the beast known as the standard workplace meeting, and it means to defeat you through wasted time and bad decision making. Recognize its signs as you work to purge it from your routine and the routines of others.

SUMMARY

- Identifying the elements of the standard workplace meeting is a basic step towards avoiding it. These components include a group of three or more people, a moderator, the sharing of real time, a loose agenda and goals, and the gathering of information.

- The flaws of a meeting include the colorful cast of quirky personalities that occupy it.

- Sometimes a meeting is disguised as something else. This camouflage makes it no more useful.

- Some get-togethers—such as those involving training, rehearsing, conventions, customer service, and pep talks—can be beneficial and need not be avoided.

CHAPTER 3

Discover the Lost Art of One-on-One Management

VISIT A THOUSAND PEOPLE—
ONE AT A TIME

Have you ever watched one of those C-SPAN reports showing the typical whistle-stop of a campaigning politician? The clip often continues ad nauseam, with the politician shaking an endless sea of hands along a mile of barricades while smiling and looking into as many sets of eyes as possible.

Politicians have it figured out. Addressing people one-on-one—even for one split second per person—translates into absolute grass-roots power, having tremendous influence on an exponentially larger number of people. There is a lasting positive impact from looking people in the eye while shaking their hand.

As a manager, encountering people regularly on an individual basis not only has a beneficial effect on their outlook towards you, but it also intensifies the personal accountability in your organization. Put simply, people respond more positively to guidance that is pointed directly at them. Addressing people one-on-one has a moving influence on individuals. It is pure, transformational leadership.

I remember my first manager, Verna, approaching me privately, with the assistant manager on-hand, when I was a very young savings and loan teller.

"Scott, do you know why you're sitting here?"

I knew. "Yes ma'am. I believe you're unhappy with my performance."

She nodded. "Can you tell me what you think has been wrong with your performance?"

I listed some of the things I thought I had been doing wrong.

Again, she nodded. "Scott, do you know why you were hired into this job?"

I was silent.

"You were hired because I think you can do it. This is too important a responsibility for just anyone. You're on this team because I think you have what it takes to make this savings and loan run well. I'm counting on you. I want you to think over those things you said about your performance and think about what you personally can do to improve. Is there anything that might keep you from doing that?"

"No ma'am."

"Well, if you think of anything, let me know. I'm here to help. Now, don't let me down. Okay?"

"Yes ma'am."

Not much to that talk, really. It was brief, to the point, without much emotion or two-way interaction. And, I dare say, she probably had used the exact same script at some point with every teller there. So why do I vividly remember Verna and that talk we had so many years ago? Because it worked. I *did* try harder, and I became a lot better at what I was doing, both technically and professionally.

Surely, it was phrases such as *too important a responsibility*, *I think you have what it takes,* and *I'm counting on you* that had such a dramatic effect. They are powerful phrases when used one-on-one. The payoff from such simple, personal expressions speaks volumes as to why it is worth the time to separately visit 1000 people.

And speaking of time, does this type of personalized leadership take *more* time than managing with meetings? My argument is just the opposite. The stories of successful meetingless managers I have known or interviewed indicate a wonderful paradox about one-on-one management: managers actually *save* time by communicating and influencing team members one at a time.

Consider this hypothetical example. Suppose you have to manage 1000 people without meetings, and you have to make it work solely from a time management perspective. You open your daily planner and proceed to devise a tight but doable business agenda.

Let's keep it simple. Use groups of 10 and suppose that you're in charge of exactly 1000 people in an organization. There are probably three levels of management, meaning 10 people are managed by one person, and those 100 first-tier managers are probably managed by 10 second-level managers—your key players. Let's assume you need to see each of your key players once a day for 20 minutes. That's 200 minutes. Figure on another 20 minutes each morning and each afternoon to meet with your administrative assistant—a total of 40.

Let's assume you would like to delve a little deeper into your colony, checking up on particularly good or bad first-tier managers. Let's say you meet with two a day, at 20 minutes each for a total of 40 minutes. Allow an hour for lunch.

In the afternoon, allocate yourself 20 minutes to answer to your superior. Assume an hour each day to address the "fires" that need putting out, and assume that you're balancing the fire fighting with one hour each day of long-term project planning. Assign 30 minutes for disciplinary or legal affairs. And, finally, give yourself 30 minutes to roam a particular department, as any good one-on-one manager would do.

The grand total? Five-hundred-and-forty minutes. That's a nine-hour day, including lunch—probably less than anyone in charge of a 1000-member organization usually puts in.

Here is what your schedule might look like.

8:00 A.M. *Review agenda/concerns with admin. assistant.*

8:20 A.M. *Discuss Department One with dept. manager.*

8:40 A.M. *Discuss Department Two with dept. manager.*

9:00 A.M. *Discuss Department Three with dept. manager.*

9:20 A.M. *Discuss Department Four with dept. manager.*

9:40 A.M. *Discuss Department Five with dept. manager.*

10:00 A.M. *Discuss Department Six with dept. manager.*

10:20 A.M. *Discuss Department Seven with dept. manager.*

10:40 A.M. *Discuss Department Eight with dept. manager.*

11:00 A.M. *Discuss Department Nine with dept. manager.*

11:20 A.M. *Discuss Department Ten with dept. manager.*

11:40 A.M. *Discuss career development with First-Tier Manager Number 1.*

Noon Lunch.

1:00 P.M. *Discuss career development with First-Tier Manager Number 2.*

1:20 P.M. *Scheduled telephone call with Regional Vice-President.*

1:40 P.M. *Edit first draft of requested capital expenditures report.*

2:40 P.M. *Consider disciplinary action for habitually tardy employee.*

3:10 P.M. *Buffer time. (Make-up time due to "putting out fires" earlier.)*

4:10 P.M. *Visit Department One.*

4:40 P.M.   *Review tomorrow's agenda/concerns with admin.*
              assistant.

5:00 P.M.   *Depart.*

What's missing? Oh, yes—the meetings. Notice how much is accomplished during this typical workday, all by practicing scheduled one-on-one management and by shunning the standard workplace meeting.

Are such managers out there—capable and influential people that pack their schedules with one-on-one meetings along the lines of this example? Yes. By most accounts, they are the exception to the rule, and their style runs contrary to the commonly held image of the executive who commands the boardroom. But they do exist and their methods are proven.

One such executive is Erik Skaggs, who has successfully employed the art of one-on-one management on two fronts. First, he is the vice-president of production and marketing for Metropolitan Mortgage & Securities Co., Inc., based in Spokane, Washington. He oversees more than $100 million each month in commercial lending, financial contract purchases, and securities sales. Instead of meeting daily with his three different staffs, Skaggs chooses conferring individually with his department managers, bringing the three department heads together only once a week for a brief overview. "Who needs big meetings when you have great field commanders?" he asks rhetorically.

Second, Skaggs is a political strategist, having run 40 campaigns over the last 15 years. In 1994, he was the campaign manager for U.S. Representative George Nethercutt (R, Wash.), the first candidate to unseat a sitting Speaker of the House (Tom Foley) in 135 years. "Sure, people have this vision in their minds of a campaign headquarters packed with committees convening strategy and policy meetings," he says. "But the truth is that any good campaign has one strong manager, meeting with workers one-on-one and then sending them out individually, with different tasks, throughout the community. Any campaign headquarters obsessed with committees and meetings is setting itself up for an Election Day loss."

HONE YOUR ONE-ON-ONE MANAGING SKILLS

Purging yourself of meetings and setting up your schedule to allow for one-on-one management is the first challenge. The second challenge is conducting the process.

One-on-one management consists of five steps.

Establish rapport

First, you must establish rapport with the other person. Rapport is harmony, mutual respect. It is the good mix of professionalism and trust that form any good business relationship.

Tom Gerding is the vice-president and co-owner of Ramsay-Gerding Construction Company in Oregon. He oversees 50 people and $30 million of construction management and general contracting projects each year—essentially without meetings. "Brief staff get-togethers might add up to an hour total per week," he says. In place of meetings, he uses what he calls an "open office arrangement"—which translates into a penchant for one-on-one management.

Gerding attributes his success at this type of leadership, in part, to emphasizing rapport and open-mindedness. "Make yourself extremely approachable," he suggests. "As long as you don't elevate yourself too much above others, and as long as you remain open to the ideas of others, you won't ever have to worry about the people around you becoming 'yes men.' You'll always tap into the special, creative talents they each have."

Managers often possess some of the ingredients for creating rapport, without actually formulating or producing it. For example, harsh bosses may hold respect, and lenient bosses may hold friendship and trust. But without the total package of rapport, one-on-one management never realizes its full potential. The reason? Much as any supervisor hates to admit it, there is usually a sizable gap between what managers want and what they *think* they want.

An example:

Joe the Boss: "Sam, let's get the machine running Order A first thing this morning."

Sam: "Okay, boss. But are you *sure* that's what you want?"

Joe the Boss: "Well, I *think* it's what I want. What's on your mind, Sam?"

Sam: "The machine is running Order D right now. It will take a lot less downtime modification to set it up for Order C, which, by the way, has an earlier shipping time. The transition from Order C to Order A is also relatively short. We could have you on Order A two-thirds into the shift, which will still get it out the door well before its drop-dead shipping time."

Joe the Boss: (Looks over the order sheet, run times and scheduled shipping times.) "Sounds good. Let's do it your way."

What just happened? Is Sam such a loyal, good-hearted employee that he felt compelled to maximize the machine's production time for his company? It's possible, but doubtful. Is Sam getting anything out of the new arrangement? Probably, especially if modifying the machine to go from Order D to Order A would have been a hassle. However, running three dramatically different orders during the course of his shift more than likely offers little consolation.

Perhaps what really just happened was that Sam was looking out for his boss. Joe probably has the unorthodox habit of asking his workers for advice on a daily basis. Sometimes he follows it. Sometimes not. But it is always asked for, and it is always considered in a serious, deferential way.

By doing it Sam's way, Joe is not only maximizing machine time; he is demonstrating respect and trust—two characteristics of rapport. Sam—and those around him—is likely to take care of Joe the next time the opportunity arises. Rapport feeds on itself.

Keep in mind that rapport is not easily identifiable. Suppose Sam had set up the orders precisely like Joe had initially dictated, without saying a word? Certainly Joe would think to himself, "That Sam's a good worker—he always does *exactly* what I ask." The rapport would not be there, and yet Joe would have no way of knowing. Sad for Joe because, as mentioned, there is usually a big difference between what managers want and what they *think* they want. Thank heaven for patient, capable employees who, through rapport, are willing to show managers the difference.

Internalize priorities

Second, you must have the worker internalize priorities. You can crack a whip as hard as you'd like. But if people in your organization are unconvinced something's important, it will never get the attention it deserves. Workers need to consider important those things *you* consider important.

Admittedly, it is possible to get some results by threatening people. A company I worked for once put out a policy letter to its employees regarding "safety lock-out," stressing the importance of disconnecting all sources of electrical power from a machine before entering it or repairing it. This three-page letter used the phrase *termination of employment*—or similar words—eleven times. It unquestionably got *my* attention! After reading that letter, the notion of climbing into a machine without first "locking it out" never entered my mind.

However, not all workplace priorities are life-and-death urgent. Besides, serious threats quickly saturate a work environment, having diminishing effects or, even worse, creating indifference and malaise.

Positive reinforcement is not the easy answer, either. Constantly rewarding adequate performance also becomes numbing, as people begin to expect prizes for all completed tasks—like a circus-performing seal anticipating a sardine with each accomplished body roll.

The most successful way to cause people to accomplish specific tasks is to have them *internalize* your priorities. That is, they need to grasp for themselves the importance of things you knew were important all along. Sometimes it takes little more than explaining to people—one-on-one—just what those things are and why you consider them meaningful. If you're sincere enough and creative enough in emphasizing the team's objectives, you'll eventually convince people why your challenges need to become *their* challenges.

Set specific goals

Third, you must set specific goals.

What dependable mind readers we sometimes expect others to be! How often do we sit silently—disappointed, hurt, upset—without sharing these sentiments with the ones who caused them? How many jobs have been lost, careers ended, with the people involved not having the slightest idea what went wrong?

For one-on-one management to work, you need to set and communicate specific daily, short-term, and long-term goals. These goals need to be written down and followed up. There should be no doubt about what is expected by whom and when.

A boss of mine once told me he missed his old job—the job I held. "Why is that?" I asked.

"Because," he said, "when I had your job, I always knew what was expected of me."

I saw his point. The greater a person's responsibility, the more ill defined the role. On the other hand, at least some of his predicament could have been attributed to poor leadership on the part of his immediate supervisor, who could have been more specific about what was expected.

Your specific goals should have clearly fixed time lines. They should be attainable. And you should define what constitutes success. People should be able to identify on their own when the goals you have given them are being met.

Consistently follow up

Fourth, you must consistently follow up. You should think nothing of saying, "Here's specifically what I need from you—and I need to see it tomorrow morning at 10:40." And then you should think nothing of asking for the results at 10:41 A.M. the next day.

Unfortunately, most workplace direction receives little or no follow-up. This is distressing. Follow-up is synonymous with implementation. No follow-up, no implementation.

All managers have grand plans, bold ideas. They usually are shared at staff meetings, complete with "butcher block" outlines, graphs, and handouts. Often, they are damned good ideas. But without implementation, those graphs might as well itemize one's favorite nursery rhymes.

When you ask something of someone in your organization, write down on your calendar a precise date and time for completion. Write down dates and times for checking up on its progress. Pronounce these dates and times, and correct the worker who dares not write them down as well. Use 20-minute blocks of time (such as 10:40 A.M., just mentioned), so that people perceive your time as tight and valuable, which it is.

Build your entire schedule around such follow-up. Who says a manager's entire day has to be filled with providing new guidance and new ideas? If 80 percent of your day simply involves subsequent action on earlier great ideas, then life is easier with its goals more easily defined.

Again, don't be afraid to ask for exactly what you need and when you need it. Write it down, and make others write it down as well. And follow up (implement), follow up (implement), follow up (implement).

It may be easy to pooh-pooh the boss who makes such demands at a meeting. Demands, excuses, misinformation—they're all part of the staff meeting game. Besides, what are a boss's options when a project is reported as unfinished? Embarrassing the substandard subordinate in front of others is bad form, and throwing a tirade is fruitless (unless you're fond of the "deer caught in the headlights" look).

But one-on-one work direction is different. It intensifies personal accountability—consistent follow-up is the fuel that provides the fervor.

Listen

You need to listen. Humans hear a lot but generally don't listen much. That's a shame, because listening is power. A manager who effectively listens increases his capacity to solve problems by a factor of 10. A manager should execute good body language and eye contact. He should acknowledge what a person is saying by repeating back some of the key phrases and ideas. He should write down important information.

Let's expand on listening.

LEARN HOW TO LISTEN

No one listens anymore. I mean *really* listens—as when an idea is transferred from one mind to another and is actually comprehended. Television and computers have destroyed our ability to concentrate. The most complicated news stories have been reduced to 15-second sound bytes. TV remote controls have "surf lock," making the television jump from channel to channel and giving the brain three seconds to absorb and analyze each selection. Search engines on the Web provide us instant access to information on anything and anyone. Online chat rooms are filled with one-sentence conversationalists, sometimes a dozen at a time, all forcing their opinions onto the screen, none seeming to understand or acknowledge or care about the other points of view. Even on Web forums, where topics are debated at length, commentators are criticized as too wordy if their arguments cannot be contained on one computer screen. If your audience has to "page down," you have lost them! The method of gathering, absorbing, digesting, and contemplating at length any type of relayed information is simply as outdated as having milk delivered to the front door.

Listening is not merely outdated. It is a lost and forgotten art. People, I believe, don't *choose* not to listen: they simply *don't know how* to do so anymore. As a result, those rare good listeners—like the keepers of any lost art—are well-regarded and can accomplish a great deal.

Begin with an easy exercise—easy to understand, but not so easy to do. For one entire day, try to let everybody you talk to *completely finish* each statement *before* you begin to formulate your response. You may be surprised how difficult it is. The brain can process words substantially faster than the ear can hear them or the mouth can say them. Consequently, most of us—especially the A-type personalities who incline toward management—presume the meanings of what a person is saying and form opinions and prepare responses, all about two-thirds of the way into the person's statement. It's as if the last third of any remark were immaterial. Thus, throughout the course of a day we lose at least a third of everything we are told. See if you can, for one whole day, listen to each thing someone tells you, one sentence at a time from beginning to end, before interpreting it or responding to it. You may be surprised at what you have been missing, and you may see fit to continue the experiment for life!

Here's another exercise—not quite so important to listening, but still significant in understanding the deterioration of conversation and concentration in many cultures. Try to spend a day responding to only *half* of what is said to you. Don't ignore people's statements. Look them straight in the eye, nod pensively, and say, "I see" or "I'll have to think about that." If it's important, write it down. Other than that—half the time—don't respond verbally. You will be amazed at how people react to you. Many times, when you don't answer back right away, people will feel unconsciously obligated to elaborate on what they have just said. In other words, if there's silence, *they* will feel a need to fill it. This elaboration could provide the important facts you need to make an informed decision. It could give you the *story behind the story*, adding a completely different twist to the person's initial statement. It seems like playing mind games with people, but it's really not. These days, when people say something, they expect an immediate response (which they only partially hear), in order to move onto their next state-ment. When that immediate response does not happen, they are left with two instantaneous options: a) stay silent and wait for a thoughtful retort (hah!), or b) keep the ball moving by expounding on what they have just said.

We have a very deep, very human desire to keep conversations moving, even if no one is really paying attention. Successful salespeople learn about this desire early on in their careers and they use it well. They are taught to play on it by always keeping the ball in the other person's court. Eventually, many people say "yes" to a salesman's visit or even the sale itself, just to get the ball off their side of the court.

If you become accepted as the rare manager who listens thought-fully, without immediately bouncing back a response, people eventually will find you approachable. Not only will you hear the *other one-third* of what people are saying, but also people will be more inclined to share with you their most important concerns and brightest ideas.

Perhaps the greatest listener in the history of humankind—or at least the greatest proponent to the art of listening—was Carl Rogers. A giant among psychologists in the 1950s through the 1980s, Rogers founded *client-centered therapy*, which was brilliant in both its effectiveness and its simplicity. Rogers advocated the notion that, by intensely listening to someone and then mirroring back the person's statements, a counselor could bring the person to understand a problem more clearly, and eventually solve it. It sounds preposterous at first—the notion of helping someone simply by hearing, understanding, and paraphrasing. And yet it works in a big way. The Rogerian method is still one of the predominant counseling techniques taught today. Listening and reflecting. It is pure, unadorned genius.

Good listening begins with body language. And good body language begins with where people confront you. When someone approaches you with a problem, it is best not to have a desk or a table between the two of you. Managers and administrators subconsciously hide behind these fortresses, and people in the organization subconsciously sense it. If you have two chairs alongside your desk—ready for conversation—you are opening yourself to a wealth of information and concerns.

Fortresses can be created with your body as well. Folding your arms or resting your hand across your mouth as people speak to you is an example of such a subliminal barrier. Again, we tend to do it without thinking, and those who speak to us react to it without thinking. As clunky as it feels at first, if you are sitting down while someone speaks to you, rest your hands flat, one on each knee. Lean slightly toward the person. If you are standing, allow your arms to hang freely at your sides. Trust me—eventually you will become comfortable with these stances. And deep down, without knowing it, people will find you more approachable.

Another important part of body language is eye contact. Eye contact is fundamental to all listening, and yet it tends to be played down. In truth, it is often avoided. The eyes are the gateways to the soul—and many of us prefer to keep our souls hidden, thank you. But you must open yourself, and exercise good eye contact, in order to be an effective leader.

Good body language also includes acknowledging what a person is saying. Nodding whenever someone finishes a complete thought is probably the most appropriate way to recognize that thought. As it is silent, it allows the person to continue.

Without acknowledging another's thoughts, you'll probably never get the full story. Also, you'll never be approached by the person as often as you should. Fortunately, there are other ways besides body language to confirm what other people are saying. The Rogerian method of paraphrasing is very effective. If someone says, "I'm not having a good day today," you respond—almost mirroring the comment—by saying, "So your day's not going well." By sending the exact thought back to the person, you allow for both a display of understanding and for a natural progression into the next thought—and the next, and the next. Remember, just as with a counselor or a therapist, the initial objective of a good manager is to get the *full* story.

You do not have to turn every problem someone approaches you with into a case study in listening or counseling. Most of the time people come to a manager they bring minor concerns or observations.

"Joe, I thought you should know the warehouse roof is leaking again along the east wall." Is this a big concern on the part of the employee? Maybe, maybe not. Should you still exercise proper listening skills as she makes the observation? You bet. First, it will show her you appreciate the information.

Second, it will say volumes to her about how you will deal with matters of greater importance in the future.

Perhaps the best, most dramatic way to demonstrate to people that you hear and understand what they are saying—items both great and small—is to write down their concerns on the spot. I am a big fan of time planners and organizers. I like the nifty coding for prioritizing time and projects. If you write down 20 things people bring to you each day, all on the same page with important appointments and urgent activities, people will appreciate the attention and equal standing. Later on, you can code and sort these items as your time and energy allows.

Developing good listening skills puts you leaps and bounds ahead of others toward discovering one-on-one management.

COMMUNICATE YOUR THOUGHTS TO ANOTHER, SINGLE MIND

You can see it clearly on a person's face—the look of indisputable understanding. Have you ever tried to communicate with someone who spoke a different language? You may have drawn a picture, or pointed out a photograph, or acted out your thought. When the person finally grasped what you were trying to say, the connection was undoubtedly and instantaneously recognizable. Faces brightened, with widened eyes and raised eyebrows and perhaps a smile and a nod of the head. A thought had been communicated to another, single mind.

There's something about such an encounter. It's pleasurable! The successful transfer of information is a gratifying experience.

So why don't we try to do more of it? Why do we, instead, choose to live in uncertainty, wondering on a daily basis if our ideas are getting across to anyone? Why do we often choose to roll in the muck of misunderstanding, rather than to walk the unobstructed, paved path of comprehension? Why do we often settle for static?

The fact is, while people find the thriving transmission of information satisfying, they also find the communication process itself curiously painful. We all have friends, relatives, even bosses who tell *others* what they want *us* to hear, hoping that it gets back to us in some quirky, gossipy fashion.

You need to endure the pain of clean, unadulterated articulation in order to enjoy its rewards. If nothing else, fully developed expression is the ultimate starting point for everything you do as a manager— setting policy, organizing projects, implementing change, supervising production, evaluating performance, rewarding success, and counseling against failure.

Follow these three steps to make the discomfort of communicating a little more bearable and the reward a little more attainable.

Make sure you know what you want

The first step to proper interaction is probably the most obvious and the most difficult. The first step is to know what you want. Know what you *really* want. How often do we begin to ask for something without knowing what it is we are asking for?

I once had a senior plant worker complain that the junior workers weren't cleaning the machine during nonproduction time. Taking the complaint at face value, I gallantly set out to get the junior workers on my crew cleaning the machine at the first opportunity. On the first try, a junior worker tore the plastic cover on a machine roll, shutting us down for a while. "Well," sniffed the (same) senior worker, "that's what we get for having junior people at this end of the machine!" Surely, this was a man who did not know what he wanted—unless what he wanted was to constantly complain!

Keep your sights set on specific personal and organizational results. Make sure these results apply to your daily and long-term goals. Have these goals written down, and refer to them often. That way, when you ask for something, it will follow the broad strokes of a big picture.

We all have known the boss who bellows many commands, most of which contradict each other. He is the ultimate buffoon, more interested in the energy generated by actions and reactions than in legitimate accomplishments that bring an organization a little further up the side of the mountain. He doesn't even know where (or what) the mountain is, much less how much more climbing there is to the top. We dare not laugh at him to his face. So we listen to the inconsistent orders, following the ones that we guess he might check up on, and ignoring the ones we hope he might forget about.

Don't be such a boss—or, if you are one, accept it and begin the change. Again, know what you want, know when you want it, and understand how it fits into the big picture.

Say it in your mind before you say it aloud

The second step to effective communication is to phrase your thought precisely in your mind before it escapes through that big opening on your face. Since the brain thinks faster than the mouth speaks, you need to ensure that you haven't moved onto your next thought before you have finished uttering your last one.

If your thought involves a request or some type of work direction, make sure you formulate it in the same way you came to decide what it was you needed. Again, say exactly what you need, when you need it, and render precisely what constitutes completion. If any follow-up is required, mention when it will take place. And finally—as you did when determining this need—relate it to the big picture.

Here's an example.

"Sam, it seems likes we have a large number of outdated parts in our supply room. What are your thoughts?"

Then, appropriately, you listen to what Sam had to say, perhaps writing down important points for later reference.

Assuming he has said nothing to contradict your initial observation, or to spur further consideration, you continue. "How's your schedule looking tomorrow? Why don't we say by tomorrow at 3:10 P.M. that you have a rough idea how much of this inventory is obsolete, along with some ideas on how to get money out of getting rid of it? If any of it falls under consignment, I'd like to know. By the end of the week, I'd like to have a specific plan for clearing the parts out. Also, let me know how many people you think you might need to help. Is that possible?"

Again, listen to Sam. Filter out the tantrumlike protesting and the cries for mercy.

Finally, the big picture: "I appreciate it, Sam. I don't know why we can't get rid of at least a quarter of what's in here. It will help cut down the amount of time people are spending in here looking for parts, and it will present less of an embarrassment the next time the auditors from corporate headquarters take a look at the place."

Now Sam knows what you want and when you want it. He knows what the follow-up will entail. He knows what establishes success. And he understands the big picture, even if he doesn't agree with it. Sound easy enough? Ask yourself how different things might have been had the same topic been discussed at a morning staff meeting. What sort of theatrics might have taken place? How defensive would the conversation have become had others been around to beat up on poor Sam? How diluted would the final instruction have become?

Take it one priority at a time

The final step to effective communication is to concentrate on one important idea at a time. You need to fight the overwhelming urge to suffocate your important employees whenever you see them.

I remember being pulled with the other junior managers into my boss's office, where he would spend an hour each morning reciting a litany of priorities and tasks. As a young, professional subordinate, I would write down every single thing he was saying.

Once, he caught me putting stars next to certain items. He asked me what I was doing.

"Well," I replied, "I'm starring the things that seem especially important."

"In that case," he said matter-of-factly, "star all of them."

Needless to say, his fire-hose method of prioritizing didn't translate well into effective communication.

Don't fall into this trap of making all things always important to all people.

Process improvement director John Frost suggests that people can absorb only one or two priorities at a time. "When someone walks away from you," he says, "you should be comfortable that the person understands one or two goals and their exact measures of effectiveness."

MAINTAIN YOUR LEADERSHIP PRESENCE

Don't lose your leadership presence as you begin to exercise the wonderful method of one-on-one management. Make certain that dealing with some people face-to-face doesn't give everyone the impression that you are immediately accessible all the time. Don't get me wrong: a good boss is an approachable boss. But being pulled aside too often can hinder your schedule. Furthermore, if everyone immediately comes to you rather than first appealing to *their* immediate supervisors, you are undermining those supervisors' authority and effectiveness.

You can avoid being too accessible without seeming condescending. When approached by someone with a quandary, ask the person, "Who do you normally go to with a problem such as this?" After you get an answer, ask, "And what did so-and-so have to say?" The presumption, of course, is that the appropriate person already has been spoken to, and that you are a next step. If this situation is not the case, ask, "Are there circumstances that are keeping you from approaching so-and-so first?" If the answer is no, then redirect that person.

You also can maintain your leadership presence by keeping one-on-one management as open a process as possible. "One-on-one" doesn't mean one-on-one behind closed doors. In fact, today's legal climate suggests that any sort of counseling or criticism should include having a third party on hand. (During Verna's guidance session with me, mentioned earlier, the assistant manager was present.) Having a third person around neither precludes nor detracts from effective face-to-face encounters. (And, for reasons mentioned in the last chapter, it doesn't automatically create a *meeting.*) On the contrary, having the right person at your side can enhance your influence. For example, during your daily walk through a particular department, bring along the next senior supervisor, or perhaps an up-and-coming manager that you are mentoring. Or bring along the department's supervisor. Many workers will appreciate the extra set of eyes and ears when they offer their input.

Finally, you can sustain a leadership presence during one-on-one management by avoiding the urge to overburden individuals as you meet with them one at a time. As you will be seeing people more often face-to-face, you may be inclined to overburden them. Ward off this compelling urge. Whenever possible, limit yourself to one important request, and therefore one success story, per person per encounter.

Remember, managers often think they need meetings simply because they believe they cannot supervise any other way. In other words, they hold meetings—in spite of hating them—because they do not have any other tools to cause a transfer of information or to cause an action. Make one-on-one management one of those *other* tools in your toolbox. Think of it as a wonderful, lost talisman, with all its enchantment and mystical effectiveness. Magically visit 1000 people in your organization, one at a time, with time to spare.

Mysteriously transfer your exact thoughts to another, single mind, time after time.

It can happen, once you have uncovered the lost art of one-on-one management.

SUMMARY

- One-on-one management takes less time than meetings.
- People respond better to one-on-one guidance.
- A manager should not use business meetings to avoid addressing people one-on-one.
- One-on-one management means establishing rapport, internalizing priorities, setting specific goals, following up, and listening well.

CHAPTER 4

Embrace the Role of Team Leader

CLARIFY WHO'S IN CHARGE

The corporate world, in many ways, is in the middle of an identity crisis.

On one hand, newspaper business sections are filled with stories about successful companies and the individual leaders behind them. Nothing gains more attention than the story of that lone visionary who either leads a corporation to great heights or takes a floundering organization and turns it around.

On the other hand, companies seem more and more determined to water down the decisiveness of their leaders and to turn leadership decisions over to an increasing number of committees and teams.

In many organizations, managers aren't even called *managers* anymore. The term has given way to politically correct misnomers such as *team facilitators* and *manufacturing resources*. The *resource* label seems especially insulting, as if managers were a commodity to be ordered in desired bulk.

I once was interviewed for a job with a major snack food distributor that embraced a concept they affectionately called "managed chaos." The interview had been set up by a corporate recruiter and seemed promising enough. I was to spend the morning going through the same screening as all the other recruits and, after lunch, I was to be checked out by upper management for a job as a second-tier production supervisor.

During the morning screenings, I spoke with several first- and second-tier managers who were quick to tell me how chaotic and disorganized their manufacturing processes were, as if boasting. They seemed quite convinced that such disarray was an indicator of their success.

"So," they each asked in one form or another, "how do you think *you'd* approach such a work environment?"

I hesitated but finally gave in to my West Point Honor Code indoctrination. "To tell you the truth," I said, "if given the opportunity, I would apply more structure and accountability to each and every step of your operation."

After a candidates-only lunch, we were each led down a separate hallway. A young manager at the site had been given the task of escorting me to my next designation. "Do you have all your stuff?" he asked.

Grabbing my briefcase and a half-filled-out job application, I responded *yes*.

Apparently, the interviewers had compared notes during lunch. This young man led me to my proper place in his fine company—the parking lot. "Good luck," he mumbled, and with a handshake, I was looking at my car. Two days later, I received a standard letter of rejection in the mail, dated the same day as my interview! (Perhaps my suit had been wrinkled.)

The unfortunate trend away from strong leadership structures seems to be gaining acceptance in academic circles as well. As a college instructor, I am amazed at how some management textbooks allude to the questionable nature of having one, strong leader guiding an organization. There exists a pervasive argument in business schools that MacArthur-type leadership is something of an asterisk to a team's performance, and that strong leaders may not have all that big an impact on organizations. The suggestion exists that any concern at all with corporate leadership has to do with an innate need to credit a specific person with a group's achievements or failures.

Perhaps even more disheartening is that many managers themselves seem to be embracing these trends. At times, it seems most people in charge don't want to be accountable—or at least held accountable—for their decisions anymore. Managers often tend to shield themselves behind corporate policies, work team resolutions, matrix configurations, and committees.

Why are today's business leaders taking on this new sport of hiding from decision making—and why are corporations encouraging it? Is it the fear of centralized power? Is it the fear of corporate or personal lawsuits? The answers aren't clear. But one thing is evident: if watered-down leadership is an objective, the standard workplace meeting is the vehicle for getting there. It's a sad, simple progression, really. The more an organization tends towards management via committees and staffs, the more meetings there are. And the more meetings there are, the fewer number of sound decisions there are.

In many ways, the situation is a vicious circle. A team dilutes the effectiveness of its leadership by gravitating towards trends of self-management. Self-management creates the perceived necessity to hold many, many meetings. Meetings further dilute sound decision making and the leadership that might have brought it about.

These trends create leadership vacuums not only by weakening the effectiveness of managers but also by dissuading good people away from management roles. When was the last time you met a great employee in your organization with an open desire to become a manager? Anecdotal evidence suggests the numbers are waning, and understandably so. If everyone in your organization has immediate access to all decision-making thoughts and input, and if everyone on a team has equal, initial say in how the team is run, then where's the incentive to assume a greater role in this group? Who wants more responsibility with nothing to go with it?

So what can you do to better clarify who's in charge? If you are in a position of influence at your organization, encourage people to take on greater, more visible leadership roles. Offer enticements. Yes, money is one of them, but people need more than money to take on management responsibilities. Incentives like empowerment, prestige, encouragement, announced gratitude, and mentoring go a long way towards filling some of your business's leadership needs.

If you are in a position to make a difference, clearly define a person's job and make it known to all exactly what a person is responsible for and who that person is in charge of. Don't be afraid to define the corporate ladder and to encourage progression up it.

If you are not in a position to make these changes, you can make a difference by always confirming your position on a team. Know your responsibilities and encourage such clarity throughout the team. Clarify who's in charge—and if it's *you*, embrace the role.

UNDERSTAND THE DRAWBACKS OF THE WORK TEAM

The *work team* structures of today don't make delineating leadership any easier. The management theories behind the *work team* concept seem admirable enough. The general idea is that multiskilled, highly flexible managers and workers come together as a self-managed team. They meet on a regular basis, creating standard operating parameters, best practices for success, and checklists for ensuring quality. The process essentially gives everyone fairly equal footing. A work team follows formulas for group problem solving and 360-degree, or circular, monitoring. Everyone has a stake and everyone—to an extent—is in charge.

On the surface, the work team seems like a system that cannot miss. If for no other reason, it seems feasible because people tend to support structures, priorities, and guidelines that they have had a hand in creating.

Furthermore, work teams serve large organizations looking to hire people with the ability to maneuver their way through several promotions. From a staffing perspective, many manufacturing companies are no longer interested in tracking a shift worker that, after 30 years, might become the next successful machine crew supervisor. Such companies are much more interested in hiring a squeaky-clean engineering student that, after 30 years, might take the corporation to newer and greater levels as the next CEO.

But where do these companies place this new, raw talent? Some of them see the merit in placing college recruits on engineering and maintenance projects. Others believe in baptism by fire, putting college grads directly with production crews. In a sense, these companies want it both ways: they want to develop their future CEOs by putting them—without experience—in charge of production operations, but they do not want to sacrifice the experience they lose by refusing to promote shift workers into first-tier management jobs. Up to a point, the *work team* concept allows companies to tap into both their young, fresh talent being groomed for bigger roles and their trusted, seasoned workers who know exhaustive details about ongoing processes.

On the opposing side, I submit the argument that the benefits of work teams do not justify the dramatic by-products they create—

by-products such as leadership vacuums and a lost sense of direction. My experience and my discussions with other managers suggest that work team structures hold so many disadvantages that they are capable of producing little else but meetings, meetings, meetings.

It's not easy finding managers who will go on record with their misgivings about the *work team* concept, possibly because of the philosophy's stranglehold on today's corporate thinking. However, Dan Bessinger doesn't mind discussing his doubts.

Bessinger is president of a corporate recruiting company in Burnsville, Minnesota, who, up until he started his own business a couple of years ago, was the general manager of several manufacturing locations. He was in charge of companies that made industrial machinery, leading groups of people between 300 and 600 strong in facilities that generated up to $100 million in annual sales. How did he react to work teams during his 20 years of manufacturing management? "Simple," he says. "If nothing was getting accomplished—and often nothing was—I disbanded them." Bessinger admits that he may have been a bit hasty in his response to unproductive, self-managed teams. "But," he counters, "when dealing with the failures of work teams, time is the one thing you don't have."

Here are the major drawbacks of work teams.

Work teams need too much time

Establishing a work team takes time—lots of it. The cross training is exhaustive and the meetings are endless. For a work team to be considered a success, the return on time invested would have to be so dramatic as to move a mountain. Perhaps that's why the people in charge of instituting work team programs, in the spirit of self-preservation, offer such incredible success stories.

Dan Bessinger is generally unconvinced by any glossy claim of *work team* accomplishment within a reasonable amount of time. "Sure," he says, "everyone feels good after a long meeting. They've generated a lot of fluff and they feel self-fulfilled. But upon close inspection, it's obvious that nothing substantive has happened. Nothing has been accomplished."

Bessinger says there are benefits to occasionally getting people together to draw out the personal experiences of an organization's members—experiences that everyone can benefit from hearing. He cautions, however, that "it shouldn't take a year."

Work teams leave too much undefined

Bringing together multiskilled people and sending them off to establish their own objectives and agendas might offer the flexibility that brings about innovation. But if success isn't clearly defined, then when does a work team know it is failing? Often, it doesn't know. Also, if individual jobs and responsibilities aren't spelled out, then the potential for idleness endures. Just because a work gap exists doesn't mean there's an eagerness to fill it. And if a team is preoccupied with establishing procedures and policies in a plethora of meetings, then indolent or indifferent workers easily can hide in a whirlwind of meaningless activity.

"Without a natural leader on hand, work teams can flounder, forever seeking a purpose," says Bessinger.

Work teams offer no incentive
for success

Another drawback to the work team is its utter lack of incentive. If everyone is equally in charge and everyone is equally responsible, who is accountable? Who gets the credit for above-and-beyond performance? Who gets the chewing out when things don't go well? And if credit and blame get spread evenly, then what's to account for different levels of pay and reward? If a manager cannot internalize in a worker the importance for getting something done continuously, it won't get done for long. And, by a work team's very nature, there is nothing for its members to internalize.

Why do people have their cell phones ring with goofy, obnoxious songs? We do it because we like to stand out as individuals—mostly in a positive light. With no distinct identity, the single member of a work team lacks the incentive to show off in a good way, much to the detriment of the organization.

Programs set up by work teams fall
by the wayside

A work team invariably experiences an atrophying of its programs. Even if fully implemented—with whips and chains in the hands of its organizers—most agendas fall quickly by the wayside. Charts are ignored, team problem-solving gives way to "putting out fires," and good old human indifference sets in. Again, the return on *work team* efforts would have to be tremendous to keep the flame burning on such tedious practices. In actuality—without incentives inside and outside the team—the returns are hardly noticeable, and the flame is quickly suffocated.

Not only do work teams often allow their programs to flounder, but they also occasionally forget the real purpose behind their activity. "If they're left alone for long periods," says Bessinger, "teams tend to lose sight of their original objectives."

There's yet another reason why work teams often are destined to fail. The *work team* structure contradicts a very real and natural element to human behavior: deep down, we all yearn badly for guidance and supervision.

UNDERSTAND WHY PEOPLE YEARN FOR GUIDANCE

Self-managing, *work team* structures not only mar the potential for great leadership, but they also run contrary to a very human characteristic that should not be overlooked. People yearn for lots of guidance.

When teaching children to resist peer pressure, many parents ask that irksome question:

"If all of your friends jumped off a bridge, would you go jumping after them?"

Sure, it's just a rhetorical question. It's meant to teach children a lesson. But what if a child said back to the parent, "Sure, I'd go jumping in after them—wouldn't you?" Might not the child be making the more truth-telling point?

If any person—child, adolescent, or adult—saw a large group of people jumping off a bridge, even to their deaths, I suggest he would at least be inclined to go chasing after them. In some cases, he wouldn't even bother asking the person in front of him what was going on.

This human condition is both a product of "nurture" and "nature." On the nurture side, as the world becomes smaller through communication and media, and as the "malling" of the world makes us all the more generic in our habits and hobbies, we are becoming more standardized in our actions, our goals, and our definitions of success than ever before. Personal, self-proclaimed independence of thought is quickly becoming something of an illusion. On the nature side, people possess an instinct towards compliance that is every bit as natural as what makes a toddler want to walk. People hold an inborn inclination to seek and follow authority.

It's not a bad characteristic. In fact, it's wonderful. People yearn for guidance the way a baby yearns for her mother's milk. Clear, undiluted work direction—when given properly—is rarely turned away. Says Dan Bessinger: "Even the best people need constant direction and positive feedback."

Compelling psychology studies have been conducted over the years that reveal the overwhelming tendency people have to take guidance from authority figures. Perhaps the most convincing experiment was conducted at Yale in the early 1960s. People were instructed to read questions to a "learner" in the next room—a person supposedly hooked up to an electronic shocking device. If the "learner" in the next room answered the questions incorrectly, people were individually instructed to administer electric shocks of increasing intensity. In fact, the "learner" was in on the experiment, and the individuals administering the "teaching" shocks were actually the subjects of the research.

Some of these experiments were filmed, and they continue to be studied by students of psychology and leadership today. I have watched some of these films, and they speak volumes on our human inclination towards obedience. With very little prodding from those conducting the sessions—nothing more than statements such as "you must go on"—people are seen dispensing what they believe are painful and, in some cases, potentially fatal electrical shocks to another person, despite the (acted) cries of pain and desperation from the next room. In one particularly disturbing taped scene, a gentleman keeps reading questions and pushing the shock button minutes after the false subject in the next room pretends unconsciousness! Depending upon the setting, between one-half and two-thirds of the people taking part in the study (unbeknownst to them) continued giving shocks for wrong answers well beyond the pretended calls of distress from the next room.

Parenthetically, the scientific ethics of these experiments are still debated today. Undoubtedly, those who took part experienced the very real discomfort of learning something disquieting about their inner natures. Watching the old tapes, one can't help but ask, "How far would *I* have gone—and do I *really* want to know?"

This human tendency surely has been rediscovered and misused over the ages. History is filled with examples of warped overseers leading their flocks towards mass murder, mass suicides, or mass hysteria.

But rather than lamenting this human condition, why not celebrate it? It's an attribute of people that can be either ignored or lauded—but not negated. There is no reason why responsible managers cannot acknowledge—and embrace—this particular trait. The bottom line is that people want to obey. Rather than gravitate towards group problem solving and meeting-centered decision making, they are much more likely to simply go where managers lead the way.

If people naturally yearn for guidance, then managers should be given the capacity to provide it in a responsible manner.

CHALLENGE THE TRAPPINGS OF THE MATRIX ORGANIZATION

If there ever was an organizational design that destroyed the notion of a leader making a difference, it is the *matrix organization*. In matrix organizations, two lines of management exist, one tying employees vertically to their normal functions, the other linking the same employees horizontally to individually assigned activities.

In such a corporate setup, people are assigned to special project teams. The arrangement promotes something called parallel idea development, with engineering, production, and marketing all concurrently immersed in an idea. Matrix organizations are often set up when a variety of specialties are involved, and when quick reaction to change is essential. The flaw in such a system, however, is its complete disregard for the chain-of-command—and its reliance on an overabundance of meetings. In a matrix organization, members answer to both *daily duty* functional managers and to the *project managers* under which they've been assigned. Project team members are still answerable to—and, notably, evaluated by—their particular department heads. Choosing whom to answer to and whose work direction is most important on any given day is enough to confuse anyone. As just noted, people want direction. The word *direction* not only implies instruction to head a certain way, but it also means the singular way in which one is headed!

It would seem, then, that the duel direction given to members of a matrix organization is something of an unsolvable puzzle.

Furthermore, for a matrix organization to stay focused and become successful—with people answering to both functional managers and project managers—members of these project teams have to handle the stress associated with their duel responsibilities. That's not an easy task, and it runs contrary to what psychologists refer to as the Equity Theory. That is, members of a project team may perceive an inequity in their current situations, as they must address immense project issues while tending to other daily duties, whereas other people in their departments (or other organizations) may not have such duel roles or concerns. Matrix team members resent being pulled away from their daily tasks without being released from their daily obligations. It is difficult for them to perform well if they believe from the get-go that they're getting a bum rap.

The best solution I've seen to the problems a matrix organization presents is a task force, something along the lines of a Key Projects Group, with members designated specifically to address new or special concerns or projects. They report to and are annually evaluated by the Key Projects Group manager, rather than the managers of their departments of origin. The Key Projects Group head reports directly to the division manager, the same as the department managers. Such an arrangement stops the friction among the competing factions, and direct reporting creates some basic reward power. Once a project has concluded or has gone far enough to be turned over to a department, the Key Projects Group moves onto the next assignment.

The forming of a Key Projects Group eases the feelings of unfairness mentioned above. Selecting Key Projects Group members—and then separating them from their normal daily duties—addresses perceptions of inequity. Also, such separation tends to increase this group's cohesiveness. For any group to succeed, it needs the strength of commitment and overriding ideals, or norms. In other words, the stronger the group convictions, the more likely a person is to be a team player.

And who sits at the center of this Key Projects Group? A strong leader, naturally—someone interested in piecing together the combined talent of several gifted idea-producers without physically taking them away from their creative settings.

MAKE A CASE FOR THE LEADER

Leadership can be derived from a number of sources. It can be acquired from a strong, clearly defined management structure. It can be characterized by the traits of the person who leads, such as expertise or access to information. Leadership can be categorized as *transactional,* where the manager sets standards, develops conditional awards, and then essentially backs off and allows good things to happen. Conversely, leadership can be labeled as *transformational,* where the manager exhibits charisma and deep, personal care for team members. The transformational leader inspires and intellectually invigorates others. Leadership can be defined by when a manager *chooses* to manage— such as when to bring about a change or sound a "call to arms"—and when that manager chooses *not* to act, allowing time and energy for those issues where the return on such invested effort is the greatest.

I subscribe to the notion that leadership, no matter how obscure in nature, is undervalued. A leader is someone who can inspire others to do the right thing, with little or no explanation as to the worker's personal benefit. When leaders can inspire others to go the extra mile for no other reason than to impress the leaders, they are worth their weight in bonus checks.

When organizations refuse to sanction leadership and responsibility (and when people are hesitant to accept it), meetings sprout like mushrooms—and more meetings mean more places for people to hide from such responsibility. Work teams and matrix organizations cannot exist without meetings—and the continued myth of effective conference room brainstorming creates and perpetuates the existence of such poor work structures. Meetings often water down a manager's leadership role, depriving people of the guidance they desire. Consequently, the lack of leadership and guidance creates an even greater perceived need for meetings! Thus, these spirals continue onward and downward.

Fortunately, the situation is reversible. Meetings become less necessary in the groups where leaders are allowed to lead. I have seen strong team and project directors turn things on a dime.

If there is any profession fully absorbed in and mesmerized by staff meetings, it is the U.S. Armed Forces. Commander's intent meetings, readiness meetings, operations meetings, training meetings, family support group meetings, officers' calls—whew! And yet, in a military culture mired in conferences, one focal point of leadership can dramatically reduce a combat unit's meeting requirements. John Shattuck is a full-time Army training officer in charge of helping National Guard infantry units to plan and carry out their military training. He has had the good fortune of serving under commanders who maintained a strong presence and, therefore, kept their meeting requirements to a minimum. Shattuck has, in turn, chosen a capable leadership presence over a surplus of meetings. For example, on a monthly basis, he is required to report on his battalion's staffing, training, and combat readiness. Rather than convene a meeting to draw together this information, Shattuck roams the battalion, forming assessments along the way. He makes a point of being on hand when his personnel sergeant is reviewing the unit's staffing or when the five company training sergeants are assembling their training plans. At every step, Shattuck's presence makes him a powerful influence—and he knows it. "It's not something unique to the military," he says. "People are more than willing to provide information and take orders when that one person is willing to step forward and lead the charge."

Does such powerful leadership translate into dictatorship? Certainly not. "Sometimes people confuse the ability to make a decision with autocracy," says Shattuck. "In fact, it's just the opposite. When people sense that an effective leader is present, they are more likely to bring forward their ideas and innovations."

Therefore, make a case for the leader whenever possible. If you are in a position where you can make a difference, strengthen the roles of the leaders in your organization. Some suggestions:

- Push your department to reward those who seek responsibility and take responsibility for their actions. See that your leaders get a bigger portion of the credit and accept a bigger portion of the blame.

- In your organization, if someone asks, "Who's in charge here?" make certain that person always gets an answer.

- Call a manager a manager—not a *resource*, for goodness sake! Titles in and of themselves may be meaningless. But a sense of prestige can be a valuable tool to a team manager. If it is within your power to change a person's title to better convey that person's stature and leadership role, then do so. If you are able to clearly define a person's job and make it known to all exactly *what* a person is responsible for and *whom* that person is in charge of, then do so. Redefining the ladder and encouraging progression up it can only help keep your team more consistent and your team's leadership ever improving.

- Cast your vote against work teams and matrix arrangements by denouncing their creation. Have each person in your organization answerable to only one supervisor. Never deny the reality of rank and standing in your organization: people might strive for it if they know it exists.

- Offer direct guidance to those who seek it, and encourage your managers to do the same. Subsequently, as leadership gains a foothold, reduce the number of meetings you hold until you reach the point where a meeting becomes the important exception rather than the omnipresent, expected event.

- Support your leaders and stand behind their decisions.

If you are *not* in a position where you can effect such progression, then incorporate the things that a manager on *any* level can do. Some thoughts:

- Clarify your own position in an organization. Know whom you are responsible for and to whom you answer. If you are answerable to two or more people of similar status, politely request to have the predicament rectified.

- Always choose to take on a special project over joining a work team. Whenever problems or special projects can be resolved without a work team getting involved, suggest so, even if it means you taking over the project yourself.
- Seek responsibility and take responsibility.
- Offer direct and sound guidance.
- Provide straightforward, solid advice to those who work for you and with you whenever it's requested.
- Create esteem for your position and positions of others. Respect the position of those above you, and carry your own standing within an organization with pride—but not arrogance.

Remember that successful managers exhibit charisma and deep, personal care for team members. A transformational leader truly inspires and intellectually invigorates others.

The worst aspect of self-managing teams or matrix arrangements is that they debilitate the true leaders in an organization. Conversely, teams that are not ashamed to orbit their activities around a powerful, competent leader have the potential for becoming strong and successful.

SUMMARY

- Every team needs a leader. That leader should be clearly identified.
- *Work team* structures and the meetings they create can hinder the potential for strong leadership.
- People naturally yearn for guidance. It should be given to them.

- Matrix organizations, where individuals answer to two or more leaders concurrently, keep people from gaining the work direction they desire.

- Organizations should define and encourage strong leadership. Managers should find ways to provide it.

CHAPTER 5

Try the Process of Organizational Channeling

UNDERSTAND THE NEED TO BOTH UNITE AND DIVIDE

Have you ever wondered how a really good manager gathers so many individual pieces of a large project and, like putting a puzzle together, creates a team's big picture?

I have observed exceptional leaders who can take complicated projects and systems involving large groups of specialists and make wonderful things happen—all without meetings. How do they do it? My suggestion is that they have learned how to both unite and divide their resources concurrently. In other words, they have figured out how to bring people's *talents* together without having to waste their time bringing *people* together.

I have formalized the process. I call it *organizational channeling*— a method for separating processes, routing responsibilities to their proper targets, consolidating results, and completing projects.

There really isn't anything wrong with the good *intentions* behind work teams and other participative management approaches. By all accounts, the opinions and experience of nonmanagement people in the workplace were undervalued for decades until team models for leadership came along. No one wants to return to the archaic, Weber-like brand of authoritarian control. Most managers today value the talents and opinions of their people.

As mentioned in Chapter 4, the problem with participative management is the circumstances it has created. Examples include unclear chains of authority, lack of rapid decision making, fear of decision ownership, and a wearing away of individual responsibility.

Therefore, the problem is how does a manager embrace the ideals behind participative management and handle complicated leadership tasks without surrendering to debilitating, communal structures?

My solution is organizational channeling, a process that challenges the grouping aspects of the more common participative management concepts. It offers dramatic potential for providing more time and better control to managers.

By using organizational channeling, managers and team members accept the notion that all of their little pieces put together results in something much bigger than the combined significance of all the individual pieces. In other words, the concept of synergy—that the whole is greater than the sum of its parts—is embraced. The difference with organizational channeling is that there's no obligation to keep everyone's eyes on the big picture incessantly.

Organizational channeling diverts, or channels, the skills and attention of individuals toward successful and time-efficient completion of separate parts of a team project. Managers maintain *direct* control over their areas of responsibility while at the same time respecting the unique knowledge and skills of each person in their organization.

Organizational channeling as a management tool possesses several significant attributes. It demonstrates a different kind of synergy between departments. It uses departmental and individual competition to the organization's advantage. It celebrates the role of the project manager. It garners much input and output without meetings or real-time communication. And it restores esteem to the notion of more traditional, vertical chains of command within an organization.

The essence of organizational channeling is that, most times, it is important NOT to bring different departments together on a project. I suggest that there is a distinct *quasi*-synergy to allowing departments to work individually on the same project, not to mention an air of productive competition when these departments work separately towards the same goal. It is *not* interdepartmental secrecy—it *is* a channeling of requirements to the departments and individuals where the work is most applicable, and then having a project manager make the final decisions and bring the project to fruition.

Organizational channeling can be applied effectively either to a team project, a large organizational project, or the general management of a group of any size. The key to organizational channeling is using techniques for separating work assignments, routing these responsibilities to their proper targets, consolidating the results, and attaining your goals. It's a straightforward and effective method with 10 steps.

UNDERSTAND THE PROCESS OF ORGANIZATIONAL CHANNELING

Organizational channeling follows a 10-step, circular method.

Step 1: Harvest individual feedback

This first step also could be labeled its last step, as the process is circular, building positively on itself through many cycles. Organizational channeling begins and ends with a leader garnering feedback from people on the team. This feedback can occur in a number of ways, including real-time visits by the leader. These visits are, if possible, one-on-one and at the place where each person works. (In other words, people should not be summoned to the leader.)

At these one-on-one sessions, the leader discusses the team's long-term objectives and possible goals to help meet these objectives. The leader talks about upcoming projects, the people and resources involved, as well as reviewing the successes of the recent past.

During this step, the leader exercises appropriate listening skills, doing little of the talking. If the feedback is being gathered by other than real-time means (such as e-mail or voice mail), it must be acknowledged, and appreciation must be conveyed.

Step 2: Establish the goals

Under organizational channeling, it is the leader—not the team—who ultimately establishes the goals necessary to meet the team's long-term objectives. The leader bases these goals on individual feedback, directives and guidance from higher levels, and personal insight.

Although it is important that team members are made aware of each of these goals, as needed, the leader requires neither a team meeting to announce these goals, nor group endorsement of the goals, nor full disclosure or prioritization of all the goals at once. The leader determines when and where the impact of individuals will be the most potent and then deduces ways to channel control of the team and channel activity towards achieving team objectives.

Step 3: Identify the means

Based on individual feedback and personal insight, the leader identifies the means by which the team goals can be achieved. The leader considers available assets—departments within the organization (subteams), individuals on the team, individuals outside the team, physical and intellectual assets, and guidance from the leader's peers and supervisors.

As the process is circular, this step also includes the reassessment of means currently in use. The leader evaluates the compatibility of individual duties and projects that are currently assigned to subteams and team members. The leader appraises the success and failures of subteams and individuals as they have performed duties and projects previously assigned.

Finally, the leader assesses the feasibility of using the means that appear available. For example, if a team member seems appropriate for a particular assignment, the leader estimates the probability of the assignment being successfully completed in light of that team member's skills and experience. This step concludes with an acceptable list of resources available for attaining the team goals.

Step 4: Departmentalize the means

Based on the means identification and feasibility assessment in Step 3, on paper the leader matches the tasks with the appropriate means (i.e., who will be performing these functions). This arranging is based on similarity of tasks, importance of tasks, and urgency of tasks. If necessary, departmentalization addresses the status of those people within the group.

Once the process is completed, the leader offers the program overview and task assignments to others for review and feedback, including peers, supervisors, disinterested members of other groups, and those who ultimately will have to complete these tasks. The leader takes their individual feedback into consideration before finalizing the program overview and task assignments.

If a department or subgroup performing some of these tasks is large enough, the leader assigns someone as the head of this unit, who then also applies the concepts of organizational channeling at the subgroup level.

Step 5: Channel the control

The leader goes about the routine of handing out work assignments and separately informing group members of their personalized tasks and obligations. If departments or subgroups exist, the head of each department is notified of her role and responsibilities. Tasks are described and levels of urgency are conveyed. Deadlines are negotiated with each team member or department head and approved by the leader. Each team member is informed of available assets and resources.

Upon review of the task instructions, each team member makes known what additional support is required. The team member informs the leader of any concerns.

The leader requests that each team member analyzes and reports the potential for success in completing each task and obligation. Candor is encouraged and rewarded. The leader addresses any predictions of less than complete success. In general, tasks are not reassigned once they have been handed out.

Step 6: Channel the activity

During this step, the leader ensures that each individual or department's actions within the group are directed towards each assigned task. Any errant energy is diverted back towards the assigned task. Team members are not discouraged from sharing information or obtaining information and advice from each other. However, they may not switch or consolidate tasks. Meetings among the team members are not forbidden, but the leader restricts meetings in the sense that the leader does not allow them to consume large amounts of time, energy, and resources. Furthermore, following the spirit of organizational channeling, the leader essentially does not sanction the meetings. For example, a leader would not sit in on a gathering of team members who have been assigned individual tasks.

Step 7: Gather input and effects

The leader monitors progress and deadlines, gathering feedback along the way. If the completion of one task depends on the successful culmination of another, the leader ensures that an appropriate sequential system is in place, and that the lines of communication between the individuals and departments involved are open.

While gathering the input and effects of the team, the leader offers encouragement, technical advice, and mentor support. When necessary, the leader counsels and corrects the actions of a department or team member.

The leader continues this process, monitoring a checklist of completed items and determining when all tasks have been completed and all responsibilities have been satisfied.

Step 8: Consolidate input and effects

The leader brings together the distinctive results of the program, ensuring that individual effects are connected where necessary to produce the appropriate aggregate outcome. The leader fills in any gaps and re-addresses any problems. At this point, all ideas, achievement, information, and material production are merged into what will ultimately achieve the group's goals.

In Step 8, the leader not only amasses results but also does so in such a way that reflects his own perspective on the project at hand. The leader has the singular role of seeing the big picture because with organizational channeling, the big picture is uniquely the leader's. In this same regard, the leader puts the finishing touches on the project—again, adding a personal bent to what already has been accomplished.

Completing Step 8 also serves as a suitable time for the leader to inform his supervisor on the progress that is being made and any obstacles that have turned up. The leader should be straightforward and unafraid to seek guidance and direction from this supervisor.

Step 9: Implement action to achieve goals

One might think that once all the tasks are complete, the leader's checklist is fully checked off, and all individual effects are combined, that the anticipated actions and the sought-after goals are basically attained. And perhaps they are. But in Step 9, the leader makes certain that these individual steps have, in fact, culminated to achieve the team's goals.

This step could be compared to running a paper machine at a paper mill. During this process, an operator sends refined wood fiber and water, called "stock," to a pressurized holding tank. Another operator controls the flow of stock over a rapidly moving conveyor and into a series of presses, where most of the water is removed. As the paper passes through dryers, another operator ensures that any appropriate surface chemicals are added, that a suitable shine is added to the sheet, and that the paper is gathering at the end of the machine on a large roll drive, called a "reel drum." Even when all the operators are doing their jobs judiciously, if there is not perfect harmony and synchronization between the operators and their distinct parts of the machine, the long, continuous sheet of paper tears, and the process is for naught.

Implementing action to achieve goals means the leader ensures that all tasks are attuned to and accommodate the outcome being sought. The leader ultimately is like the conductor of an orchestra, making sure not only that the musicians know their parts, but that when they bring all their parts together, beautiful music is heard.

Step 10: Assess the results and repeat the process

The leader assesses the results of the project and the processes that brought it about. Those processes leading to success are recorded, as are those processes that have not. The leader reports this assessment to all parties involved as well as to anyone who might require or benefit from the information.

The leader appraises the performance of individual group members, departments, and subgroups, again making note of the people whose tasks were accomplished at or above the level of expectancy and noting those people whose performances merit future attention and guidance.

The leader evaluates the project for its conformity with the method of organizational channeling. Did the leader utilize methods for separating the processes within the project? Did the leader route responsibilities to their proper targets? Were results properly consolidated? Were goals attained? Were procedures properly documented?

Finally, the leader seeks the feedback of individuals on the team, hoping to learn from their experiences and triumphs. The leader asks each member for a self-assessment. The leader asks each member for ways in which that member's tasks might have been more easily achieved. The leader asks if, indeed, the task itself was appropriate to accomplishing the goals of the group.

By seeking this feedback, the leader brings the process of organizational channeling back to Step 1.

UNDERSTAND THE SYNERGY OF SEPARATENESS

Throughout the process of organizational channeling, the manager assigns and disseminates information separately. Heads of departments or subgroups are individually counseled on their roles in supporting the group. Individuals are given separate sets of priorities and are asked to approach their duties with differing levels of urgency. Available resources are offered to individuals in different ways, with unique mixes. The leader asks for analysis and updates from each member on distinct tasks. In sum, organizational channeling celebrates an argued *power* of separateness and, again, rests on the notion that it is important *not* to bring different departments together on a project.

Why does power exist in separation? First, it keeps group members and departments focused on individual components of a project. Rather than enduring a dilution of energy and ideas at meetings, people are able to point a laser beam of concentration on the tasks most urgent to them. Second, when tasks are assigned by the leader, group members do not find themselves wallowing in a pool of uncertainty, such as that of the muddled priorities that many times come out of free-formatted *work team* meetings. Separation of assignment is the guiding hand many group members yearn for in a work environment. Finally, separation is power because the activity and ideas and innovations produced are as distinct as the tasks themselves. In the sense that separation allows people to concentrate their productiveness on fewer, more clearly announced and defined objectives, separation is not incapacitating, but rather, it is empowering.

Bear in mind that there need not be any secretiveness or concealment to this selective dissemination of responsibility. A leader is not obligated to explain all reasoning behind all task assignments, but she should be able to openly discuss who was given what task, as well as what general inclinations prompted these assignments. If, for example, a group member is allocated a smaller budget than that of other members, it is reasonable for that member to argue for an equal (or larger) budget. The leader should be capable of clarifying the inequity of spending support, while—if the member's argument is strong enough with adequate quantitative reinforcement—also be open to the idea of changing it. But the worst, most damaging scenario would be one where the leader secretly earmarks financial backing for specific tasks, asking each member to keep quiet about the support they are each receiving.

One might argue that the lack of meetings in establishing a group vision and agreed-upon group goals takes away the synergy that exists in a pure work team environment. That is, the argument might be that with separation of tasks, the "whole" simply equals the sum of it parts. However, anyone making this contention fails to see the distinct *quasi-synergy* that exists when departments are led to work individually on the same project. Here is why.

Did you ever hear the parable of the six blind men who find the elephant? In the mid-1800s, John Godfrey Saxe told the story of six blind men who approach an elephant from different sides. One of the blind men, touching the elephant's ear, is convinced he is standing by a giant fan. Another, rubbing the tail, says he feels a strong rope. Yet another, touching the elephant's tusk, says he is next to a sharp spear. It is the reader, holding an understanding of the entire elephant, who comprehends the big picture.

But have these blind men detracted from the proper vision of an elephant, or have they *contributed* to it? Stretching your imagination, think of an elephant actually fanning someone with its ears. Or pulling something with its strong tail. Or using its strong tusks to cut or lift something. Would six people with eyesight have come up with any of these roles for the elephant? Probably not. Holding a meeting and reaching a consensus, six "seeing" men would have concluded that they had an elephant on their hands—big, cumbersome, and burden-some. What did the blind men see?—a fan, a rope, a spear, and so on. At *that* point of perception, the elephant has taken on many more roles and purposes. In other words, as these differing insights are gathered, the elephant as a whole is greater than the sum of its parts—which is the very definition of synergy. Just like the reader of the parable, who presumably can see the big picture, the leader of an organization must take the input of individuals working on separate tasks and apply their new perspectives to the big picture as the leader recognizes it.

There's an old saying that people need to "see the forest from the trees." I go one step further. I say that when people are encouraged to each look at a different tree within the same forest, their differing views, once combined, are likely to define the forest in ways it has never before been characterized. Again, at that point, the whole forest becomes greater than the sum of its individual trees. Synergy has taken place.

Organizational channeling does not devalue individual contribution to a cause. It celebrates the individual! Organizational channeling allows people to work separately, interacting when necessary without getting trapped into a group identity. It allows for personal achievement and reward. Quality assurance engineer Tracey Richards agrees. "People who are too reserved to come forward in a group often have great, individual perspectives," she says. "Once they're pulled aside, their creativity blossoms. If encouraged, they *really* develop these unique outlooks, and the group benefits."

So how does a leader take advantage of the synergy of separateness? Probably the best way you can tap into the benefits of this phenomenon is to keep your own closed mind from getting in the way. You do not have the benefit of isolating the tasks from each other in order to expand on their solutions. Mentally, all the parts of a project sit there in your mind, their parameters bleeding into each other and producing all the subjectivities that stifle creative thinking and intellectual openness. In sum, you see "the whole elephant," and necessarily cannot break up this vision in your mind. As a result, the tendency exists to filter the solutions and innovations that come back from members within the group. You must fight this inclination at all costs in order to reap the full advantages of sending people off separately and channeling their singular intensities into new discoveries.

Take advantage of the synergy of separateness by nurturing the condition along. In this regard, you serve two distinct but connected roles. First, you serve as facilitator to the group. That is, you act in such a manner that others perceive you as the one with the vision, as the focus for change within the organization. Transformational leaders are inspirational and consumed with ideals and goals for the group. If successful in this role, you really do evoke emotions in the members of your group. A transformational leader elicits loyalty from the group members and dedication of the group to its goals and causes.

In the second distinct but equally transformational role, you nurture the synergy of separateness along by displaying unwavering belief in each group member. Each member is coaxed to view a task from his own unique perspective, and to seek working solutions no matter how unusual or away from the norm or "outside the box" they might first appear. You encourage group members to each take a stand and take risks. Individuals are encouraged to confront the status quo—to confront "reality." You carry these unique solutions further by advocating a long-term learning process in each group member. Finally, you empathize with each group member as these solutions are sought, understanding the member's needs and feelings.

Another way you augment this quasi-synergy is to encourage a healthy, inherent competition among people or departments. The key is to orchestrate—or *channel*—this competition and utilize it to the group's advantage, without corrupting group camaraderie or undermining sentiments of goal ownership.

USE COMPETITION TO YOUR ORGANIZATION'S ADVANTAGE

To say that there is no internal competition within a group is folly. All energetic and enthusiastic workers eventually endeavor to have their viewpoints heard over those of others, their ideas applied over those of others, and their projects given resources over those of others. However, when the leader is established as the focal point of influence with limited time and attention to go around, and when departments or people are not working as a large team but rather as semiseparate entities, a more intense level of intergroup competition inherently takes shape. The key for you is to keep this competition healthy and productive.

Certainly the first step to properly utilizing competition between departments is to embrace it—not an easy thing to do. While competition is the bedrock of business, being anything other than harmonious and agreeable within an organization is practically anticultural nowadays. The term *politically correct* implies the appropriateness of being all things to all people, and ruffling the feathers of no one. However, little is attained in a situation where geniality is sought above all else and everyone seeks the path of least disruption. Conflict among groups ultimately must be seen as an appropriate source for finding solutions and accomplishing productive changes.

Through organizational channeling, you not only channel individual energies toward appropriate parts of a project, but you also channel competition in ways that move your group forward. The conflict must remain proactive and constructive—not degenerative. The conflict must be one part of the overall group dynamics scenario and not the entire focus or preoccupation of your group. Competition must remain balanced, without one person or department's view taking over. It must include compromises and sacrifices, rather than simply having one person's priorities gain attention at the expense of another person's.

The nature of organizational channeling offers a certain convenience when it comes to properly integrating conflict. Just as the mechanics of free enterprise are such that they tend to be self-forming and self-sustaining, the inherently detaching nature of organizational channeling tends to intrinsically draw the lines of battle where they are most beneficial. That is, by leaving a country's economy alone, a nation's leader is basically acquiescing to free enterprise. Likewise, by leaving individuals within a group alone to work on their own distinctive tasks, you are allowing productive competition to manifest itself.

Here's an example. A friend of mine, Rich Vincz—whose experience includes nearly 20 years as a supply chain manager with Dupont—was in charge of a small group of administrators. The group had recently undergone a reduction in head count. Rich decided to allow the remaining group members to determine their own work duties within this downsized department. Competition played a big role in this scenario, as these people vied for available work hours, responsibilities, and overtime allocation. Each member made a case—not only to the leader, but also to other members of the group—for assuming certain duties and working a particular block of time. Each member then made a case to the leader for taking on a certain amount of overtime hours. In this situation, overtime hours were desired but scarce in that the organization was attempting to reduce extra time worked. Since only a limited amount of overtime was to be allocated, the members understood that they were competing for the hours.

Did the situation descend into backstabbing and hard feelings, or perhaps a lack of enthusiasm and high absenteeism? No. In fact, just the opposite occurred. Rich was surprised to find that much of the competition and haggling took place *before* the specific requests for duties, time slots, and overtime came to him. That is, when group members finally put in for specific duties and hours to work, their requests did not clash, but instead conformed nicely to his schedule and list of tasks. Their combined overtime hours did not exceed his desired limit. And most importantly, the duties they had each requested appropriately suited the talents and strengths of each person. Clearly this is an example of anticipated conflict between competing workers remaining proactive rather than regressive. The conflict evidently was a primary part of this group's dynamics but was not preoccupying or hindering to the group. As Rich approved the duties, time slots, and overtime requests of each worker, the outcome of the competition certainly appeared balanced—in that one person did not seem to walk away with everything. The end result appeared to be a script for compromise.

Had the competition for duties and scheduled work time fallen off into internal bickering or unresolved confrontation, it would have manifested itself in the form of complaints and bad feelings. And, of course, there was the possibility that individuals could have requested the same duties and time slots, leaving Rich with the deciding vote. But in either case, Rich would have to do no more than what he had braced himself for, and really, no more than what is expected of any successful manager. At is turned out, just handing over the responsibility of deciding duties and work times individually to each worker was all this manager had to do to create a scenario for positive competition and eventual agreement.

Rich's case in point is clearly one where competition among individuals revealed itself in a valuable and fruitful way.

This example begs an important question. As noted, since the workers came to the group leader with duties and work hours already earmarked in their minds, it can be assumed that these members of the group had met either one-on-one or in smaller groups to work out these issues before approaching him individually. In light of this presumption, the question is, if the leader anticipates that members of the team will collaborate on problems and tasks assigned to them separately, why not simply schedule a meeting or meetings to recognize this need for correspondence?

Of course, the question is a loaded one, as it suggests a return to the work team setup—meetings and all—that organizational channeling seeks to dispute.

Why shouldn't a leader schedule meetings where competition and collaboration can take place? Perhaps the appropriate answer to this question is a counterquestion. What would have happened in the above scenario had the leader placed the members in a room and said, "Here are the group duties. Here are the time slots. Here is the amount of overtime hours I am willing to allow. Work it out among yourselves and let me know what you come up with." Would the meeting have been productive? Would the leader have seen the same positive results?

It is the contention of this commentary that the successes this leader enjoyed resulted in the fact that a) the assignments to determine duties and hours worked were handed out separately and individually, and that b) the collaborating that took place happened informally, unrecognized, and without prompting from the leader. The bottom line is that, in the separateness of organizational channeling, there is nothing wrong with behind-the-scenes alliances and collaborating, until the very second it becomes "officially" recognized or formalized.

Going back to the earlier analogy of capitalism: one of the earliest forms of capitalism was bartering, where people exchanged goods and services for the goods and services of others. The practice is still very popular today as, say, a dentist provides free checkups and fillings to the plumber who replaces the dentist's water heater. Bartering is so popular, in fact, that the Internal Revenue Service has had to become more vigilant in its taxing. But what would happen if the federal government were to force the dentist and plumber to sit together—along with other providers of goods and services—and coerce them to work out a formal bartering program? Would such a program get accomplished? Would it be encompassing? Would it flourish? Many an economist would answer "Probably not." The inherently impromptu and independent nature of bartering is what makes it so popular and successful. And in a similar light, it is the intrinsically unregimented ways that separate factions in an organization compete and negotiate that produce the successful outcomes discussed.

In sum, the group leader practicing organizational channeling needs to accept and embrace competition within the group, channel it in ways that benefit the group, and allow collaboration to take place without formalizing it.

KNOW YOUR VARIED ROLES WITHIN A CHANNELED GROUP

Leaders considering the concept of organizational channeling probably will be more worried over their own role than in any other aspect of the process. In a survey group of 56 managers asked to review this method, many of them voiced concern over the concentrated burden placed on the group leader. Some of their comments:

"Organizational channeling sounds like a good process, but it also sounds like a lot of responsibility is put on the leader to coordinate everything."

"It seems that the manager will spend more time overseeing the process than in solving the actual problem."

"Sometimes I don't want to do all the leading."

"Organizational channeling seems to call for a lot of planning, organizing, leading, and controlling."

"My reaction is that, as a manager, I do not have time for all of this baby-sitting."

Fear of too much coordinating, overseeing, leading, controlling—even baby-sitting! These are all understandable concerns. And admittedly, the group leader *is* organizational channeling's center of focus, although arguably no less responsible or visible than in any other management arrangement. Fair or unfair, there is a propensity for attributing the success or failure of an organization almost entirely on its leadership. Managers have little choice but to accept this inclination and work within its confines. When you choose organizational channeling, you not only accept this center of focus but, in fact, you embrace it. And by seizing this locus of control, you acquire a number of varied roles, each of which requires some time and attention. These roles include your portrayal as a talent scout, a coach, and an umpire. They include the roles of delegator, consolidator, and technical director. They include the roles of psychologist, motivator—even icon.

When discharging the various leadership requirements of organizational channeling, you find yourself playing the part of a one-person baseball management staff. As a talent scout, you scour the countryside, looking for the next great slugger, understanding that effective assets are available both inside and outside the team. Perhaps if these assets are not an immediate part of the team, some recruiting or trading must take place. The talent scout is always on the lookout for new physical and intellectual assets. Furthermore, as the team plays its sport, the talent scout must continuously re-appraise the successes and failures of the individual talent currently on hand.

As a coach, you assign the players to their field positions. You hand each player a work assignment and separately tell each player of his personal tasks and obligations. Perhaps team captains are assigned and given their own sets of expectations. Tasks are specified, levels of urgency are communicated, and deadlines are discussed. Each team member is provided the assets and resources necessary to play hard and win the game. The coach ensures that the actions of each player on the team are directed towards that player's specific position and capacity for team success.

As umpire, you ensure that players are going about winning the game in a proper manner. The umpire keeps players focused on fairness and their own part in serving the team. A ball player's errant energy is diverted back towards the task and the game. If players conflict in an unproductive way over whether a ball is fair or foul, the umpire makes the call and ensures that any additional conflict is channeled productively toward the game.

Through organizational channeling, you serve as a delegator, a consolidator, and a technical director—roles usually acted out by different people within a group. As a delegator, you appoint responsibility and allocate assets, serving as the ultimate clearinghouse of physical and intellectual resources. It is perhaps in this role that you not only carry the fundamental principle of organizational channeling the furthest, but also have the greatest potential for impact. Just as the story-book matchmaker ignites the most energy by matching the most compatible man and woman, the perceptive delegator gains the greatest initial thrust for a project by matching the most compatible person and task. There is no reason why a collective of properly matched people and designations cannot run themselves once assignments have been handed out.

As a consolidator, you gather feedback and results the way a cook might gather shopping list items for an exquisite meal. You ensure that results are not only attained, but are harmonious and, if necessary, in sequence. Here is another role where you can have tremendous impact. You garner and assemble results in a manner that reflects your take on a particular situation, making the solution decidedly yours. You are the one who understands the broad strokes on the canvas because the painting essentially reflects your singular vision. Furthermore, as each group member may provide one of those broad strokes, your refinements—small brush strokes or airbrush enlightening—continue to produce a portrait that merits your signature and style.

As a project unfolds, you also serve as a technical director, offering technical support and the encouragement of someone experienced in a special discipline. Managers are often portrayed (perhaps accurately) as imprecise but motivated generalists who simply administer the work of technicians. Such a depiction runs counter to the West Point Principal of Leadership #2: "Be technically and tactically proficient." Counseling and correcting the actions of others from a position of knowledge contributes to the impact of an effective multirole leader. Understanding a problem from a learning and science standpoint allows you to fill in any gaps and to smooth over any speed bumps. Furthermore, technical knowledge allows you to culminate all ideas, information, and achievements into a more focused design for attaining goals and achieving success.

These various roles are to be played neither *always* concurrently nor *always* chronologically. Some parts will be played at the same time. Some will only show themselves when necessary—if necessary. There are those managers who sometimes say, "Well, today I have to put my disciplinarian hat on," or "Today, I have to put my counselor hat on." The successful channeler wears only one hat with many, ever-changing, repositioning feathers.

Keep in mind that serving more roles does not have to translate into more time (a fear hinted at by the survey group). The entire notion of organizational channeling is one of maintaining *more* positive control with *less* time. Perhaps this indicates yet another role you have to play— that of time manager. Time management falls back on the oldest lesson of mankind, that total freedom also means total responsibility. It is easy for, say, a production shift supervisor to throw his hands up and say, "Gee, I was at meetings all day—either getting together with my work team or facilitating the brainstorming session of another work team." When your schedule is dictated by such mandated get-togethers, the time choices you make are limited and, therefore, apparent. As more freedom from meetings demands more responsibility and more required planning on a personal level, it is reasonable for you, assuming a greater number of roles, to feel more time burdened when in fact there is more time available. The triumphant leader considers the time requirements of each role, allocates the workday appropriately, and goes about the business of fulfilling these diverse expectations.

SUMMARY

- An effective team is united in its mission while its members are divided by their individual assignments.

- The steps for Organizational Channeling are:
  1. Harvest individual feedback.
  2. Establish the goals.
  3. Identify the means.
  4. Departmentalize the means.
  5. Channel the control.
  6. Channel the activity.
  7. Gather input and effects.
  8. Consolidate input and effects.
  9. Implement action to achieve goals.
  10. Assess the results and repeat the process.

- Organizational channeling celebrates an argued *power* of separateness and a *quasi*-synergy of separateness, when people and departments view a project from different perspectives and the organization benefits.

- Separated people and departments are naturally more competitive. A manager should work to keep this competition healthy and productive.

- The manager of a channeled group accepts a variety of roles, including the role of delegator, consolidator, motivator, technical director, and model.

CHAPTER 6

Get Comfortable with Delegating

UNDERSTAND YOUR FEAR OF DELEGATING

"If you want something done right, you've got to do it yourself."

Maybe so, but if you do it all yourself, you'd better expect to go through life with way too much on your plate.

If organizational channeling becomes an effective, new tool for assigning people their work, why not let old-fashioned delegating become a practical way of assigning people some of *your* work?

Managers often hold meetings because they see themselves using other management approaches ineffectively. Their tendency not to delegate goes one step further—they're afraid. The manager that fears delegating is the first to call another meeting.

Delegating is the act of authorizing and entrusting to others something that you are responsible for completing. As a management tool, nothing beats it. Any successful leader must be comfortable authorizing and entrusting to others something that he, himself, is ultimately responsible for completing. Says Army training officer John Shattuck: "You can delegate authority, but you can't delegate responsibility."

On the surface, you would think that delegating and holding meetings might go hand in hand. What better place, you might ask, than at a staff meeting to pass out assignments and projects and then, at future meetings, to hear back on the progress of others?

That answer is that delegating does not take place effectively at meetings—nor should it. If meetings were brief, focused events aimed at nothing more than assigning delegated duties, then there might— *might*—be some sort of return on the time invested in having them. But for reasons already covered, meetings never will be simple happenings. They can't be.

Holding fewer meetings—or no meetings at all—means exercising more one-on-one management. Accordingly, one-on-one management means more delegating. So, rather than being the focal point of meetings, delegating is much more beneficial as one of the instruments for *replacing* meetings and freeing up your time as a manager.

Furthermore, the *quasi*-synergy of separateness suggests that delegating is best administered privately rather than in a room filled with people.

So, if delegating reduces your need for meetings, why are you avoiding it? Why might you even fear it?

It's worth noting that one of the inherent human traits inducing managers to hold valueless meetings is also the same trait that makes managers avoid delegating. Managers possess an inner belief—deep down in their gut—that if everyone's around, all at once, and information and work guidance are being dispersed, then something actually is getting accomplished. On the other hand, delegating, like the absence of meetings, means that everyone is *not* around all at once. They're out and about—not immediately available—getting things done. That circumstance scares the hell out of many managers. They simply can't cut people loose to accomplish great things on their own.

Also, you may dread to delegate because task assigning wrongly feels like sacrificing power, and the loss of control is a scary endeavor. This is a natural and important concern. Nearly every phobia known to mankind involves the root fear of losing some type of control. Fear of delegating is compounded by the reality that even though you might delegate a task, you're still responsible for its outcome. Nothing is worse than discovering the incompetence of the people you handed assignments to through the embarrassment of their failures. It seems much less risky simply to complete a project yourself than to chance turning it over to an unknown talent. After all, at least you know what *you're* capable of achieving.

You may hesitate to delegate because delegating takes time, especially when first learning how to do it. Deciding which jobs can be handed over to whom, keeping track of their progress, reviewing their results, offering feedback—who needs it?

The answer is *you do!* If properly administered, each minute of time you spend delegating translates conservatively into four minutes of time for yourself. If you've convinced yourself that you don't have the initial minute to invest, then you'll never reap the profit of three extra minutes.

Where does that profit of three minutes come from? Simple—they come from not having to monitor every phase of every aspect of running your team. As officer John Shattuck puts it, "You don't have to constantly direct a ship if it's headed in the right direction."

You may be afraid to delegate because—as many of us do—you may truly believe that the only way to get something done right is to do it yourself. We've all been burned trusting other people to help us out. "*Go* with what you *know*," we're taught as managers—and what could be more of an *un*known than the skills and dependability of other people? Asking subordinates to do our bidding for us is uncomfortable; criticizing them for doing a poor job is even more so.

Besides, most people become managers because they're comfortable with their own skills. As a manager, more than anyone around you, you're in tune with your capabilities and limitations. You settle into the routine of doing things yourself. You go with what you know, and you *know* you'll do the job right the first time, while others will need prodding, supervision, and second chances.

You may hate to delegate because you enjoy being where the action is, and you wrongly perceive that delegating runs contrary to hands-on management—that delegating somehow means losing touch.

Fear of losing control, fear of embarrassment, fear of time constraints, fear of leaving the comfort of your own capabilities, fear of losing touch—these idiosyncrasies all seem so very human. So how do you fight these natural tendencies?

As with all the inhibiting human traits mentioned up to this point, you must first own up to them in order to overcome them. Once you acknowledge the personal inhibitions that make you inclined not to delegate, you can move on to studying the possibilities presented by delegating. Then, if you can learn to accept how the benefits far outweigh its drawbacks, you can start taking advantage of delegating as an important management tool.

PRACTICE DELEGATING

Once you've confronted your fear of delegating, take on the challenge of deputizing a few people and putting them in charge—without giving up ultimate control.

Here are some ways you can bring yourself to a point of empowering others to do the things you used to do on your own.

Take small steps at first

I generally embrace the philosophy that you should jump into a pool rather than wade into it. Similarly, some professional counselors are proponents of immersing people with phobias into the things they fear, such as forcing someone with claustrophobia to ride an elevator for a day, regardless of the initial reaction. However, there's also a different theory of knowledge among mental health professionals that advocates the incremental approach to curing apprehension. An example would be bringing someone who fears heights within the proximity of a cliff, and getting that person comfortable with the setting over time, before approaching the cliff to look over. Considering the apprehension that comes with first-time, full-scale delegation, perhaps the latter approach to entrusting others is more suitable for getting started. That is, take a few baby steps as you're learning to walk.

Begin this new, wonderful habit of delegating by making a list of those people whose expertise you can draw from. Then check your daily planner for this week's projects. Also, make a list of those likely upcoming projects. Match your team members with the appropriate scheduled work.

Find a project that is not too involved, preferably one that should take no longer than a day to complete. Make it an easy job to evaluate— one that you know a lot about.

Later that day, assess the performance of the person who performed the assignment. Was it accomplished? Were the results to your satisfaction? Provide feedback as if the person has always been expected to perform such tasks. If the job was done well, make a point of letting that person know.

From there, proceed with another task and another person on the following day. Continue assigning projects that will take a day or less to complete. This way, you can gain a quick awareness of who performs well with entrusted responsibility and who does not. Again, the key is to treat delegated work as if it always has been expected of the person carrying it out. Don't let poor performers off the hook. Counsel them as if they were not doing their regular work well.

As you become comfortable with one delegated project per day, move on to two projects per day, and then three. Then begin handing out assignments that take longer than a day to complete, or assignments involving several stages of completion. Be sure to check up on the progress at each stage. Soon, delegating will become your custom rather than the uncomfortable exception.

Assign projects rather than routine duties

A project, in this case, is defined as a relatively short-term undertaking with a beginning and an end. Limiting your delegating to duties of restricted time and scope has practical and personal benefits.

On the practical side, delegating projects—and not normal duties—helps you stay in command of the situation. Projects-only delegating is easier to keep track of. It avoids checking off a continuous laundry list of daily items. More importantly, if you try to run contrary to this practice and delegate your daily duties, you'll begin to lose the time advantage delegating provides as you work to stay updated. The beginning and ending of a project are the appropriate bookends to organized delegating.

On the personal side, delegating projects keeps you from gaining a reputation for pawning your job onto others. I vividly remember a manager whose job description included three distinct areas. His strategy: hire three temporary administrators and place each of them in charge of an area! Perhaps he was a management genius—but I think his love for early tee-off times had more to do with his massive handing over of duties. In the end, I believe it hurt his reputation.

Limiting your delegating to projects only is a tall order. Most managers would much rather tackle the nonroutine stuff and turn the mundane chores over to other people. But on balance, delegating projects and tending to your own repetitive chores will win favor and garner better performance from your team. If your description entails too many repetitive chores, make a case for having your job description changed. It might not be too outrageous a request: senior managers get aggravated when they see junior managers running around and performing routine tasks instead of tackling big-picture responsibilities. Your superior might free you from some of that monotony without your having to pass it on.

Set the example before assigning the activity

It's important that you complete a task competently at least once before you turn it over to someone else as a project. You don't need to accomplish it in expert fashion, but just well enough to understand the time, energy, effort, and brainwork involved.

Performing the activity before handing it over creates the notion among your team that you're a team member—and a team player (something that many bosses are not). I believe that you shouldn't ask anything of others that you wouldn't do yourself. Now I'm not suggesting that you pick up a broom and sweep alongside the cleaning lady—but, then again, maybe I am! Many a time, after eight hours of managing a machine crew, I would leave the plant covered with more grime than anyone else was wearing. When you delve into a task normally performed by others, chances are people will be help you along and show you the right way. Odds are you know less about the mess you've gotten yourself into than anyone else around you does. But after the job is done, people will at least know you have an appreciation for their work. Tackling a job before delegating it may seem like a small thing, but it's not. A leader who can relate to what her team has to go through is a treasure.

Performing the task competently in front of others lets your team know that you not only have empathy for what they're doing, but also that you have an *understanding* of what they're doing. There's a difference.

Utilize people based on their particular talents

Shame on the weak-minded manager who surrounds himself with weaker, subservient minds in order to make him feel more powerful. Hail to the manager who chooses talented, surefooted people for his team and then assigns them projects accordingly.

It boggles me how, as adults, we often stray from those survival tactics we learned as youngsters. When you were team captain of a neighborhood stickball game, whom did you select first when choosing teammates? In all likelihood, you picked the kids who could whack the ball the hardest, or run the fastest, or throw the ball the hardest. Many times, you would hope to win the coin toss for choosing first so you could pick the kid who stood out among everyone else. Whichever team got the *star* would do great things that day.

Did it matter that these first-picked kids could hit harder, or run faster, or throw harder than you? Of course not. As captain, your mission was clear: choose the best players and use them where they would do best. Moreover, you would have been chided had you chosen kids strictly on their willingness to follow you as captain.

Hopefully, most of us are not so egotistical as to surround ourselves with people weaker than we are. But I would argue that we often choose people based on factors other than raw talent—including geniality and a willingness to follow. I would also suggest that, as managers, some of us are loath to acknowledge, compliment, and utilize performance that exceeds anything we could have done.

Rather than deny such exceptional performance, you should celebrate it. You should lobby hard for a team with talent greater than your own. You should utilize those people on projects where their performance will reap the most fruit. And you should acknowledge and reward their successes as often as possible.

And if you're not in a position to select the stars, learn the special talents of those people already on your team. Each of us has many gifts, and any organization needs a diversity of talent. Bring yourself to the idea that each person you work with can do at least one thing better than you can do. Seeing people that way will always make you stronger as a manager. And you'll always win at stickball!

Maintain your delegating in a daily planner

A calendar book or electronic planner helps start the initial process of delegating because it's where you first go to gather projects you'd like others to complete. Write down those projects that you'd like to delegate. When you hand a project to a person, annotate this contract in your calendar book. Assuming you're at the point of delegating longer-range jobs, have a specific date in mind and mark down when you'd like to see completion or some type of progress on this project. Advise the person of the date and specifically what you expect by this time. Make certain the person sees you jot his name down in the calendar book on the date you're going to be back in touch seeking results.

Use the planner to keep track of upcoming projects that haven't yet been delegated.

Ideally, you're looking for just enough delegation, involving a comfortable number of people and activity, to warrant your keeping track in a calendar book. A daily planner provides a degree of formality to a process that, if left unmapped, becomes disheveled and ultimately forgotten or abandoned.

More importantly, the presence of a planner lets others know—perhaps subconsciously—that they cannot let these projects fall by the wayside. If you give them specific dates when they'll be asked for progress reports, and then write down their names on your planner in front of them, they will understand what has just taken place. At this point, they will know that the delegated work has become a bona fide expectation. Remember: there is freedom in structure. In this case, the structure is the calendar book marking a beginning and an end. The freedom is how people will use their innovation, energy, and creativity in accomplishing the projects you've given them. What great successes you'll see them achieve.

Encourage individual responsibility and team support

Members of an organization often settle into their own little worlds, doing their individual tasks and viewing happenings in the organization without understanding their repercussions—the ripples in the water.

Again, you shouldn't feel obligated to advertise the big picture to everyone all the time. It violates the synergy of separateness. But people should maintain an awareness and respect for the idea that there is something going on around them that's bigger than each one of them and that each of them should each be contributing to this bigger thing—this TEAM thing.

My suggestion for maintaining a feeling of both *individuality* and *team* is to let people know what is happening one or two steps before and after their actions. I was once in charge of gathering up all the rejected production from previous manufacturing shifts and repairing the mistakes so it could be shipped. Each product we received was rejected by the quality control folks for different reasons—mislabeling, mixing different products on one shipping pallet, poor packaging, damaging while moving, and so on. Rather than simply assigning the repair jobs to my team, I would tell them why a product had been mislabeled or damaged. Then I would explain how we were trying to prevent the error from happening again. Finally, I would tell them what our quality record was with this particular customer.

"Scott," other managers would say in disgust, "you're wasting your time telling them all that. All they need to know is what they need to fix."

I didn't argue, but I also didn't stop sharing with my team the one step back and the two steps forward in this quality process. I have no quantitative support, but I believe people appreciated knowing how their piece of the puzzle fit, and that they came to address their job as part of a bigger, team picture rather than one person repairing one damaged pallet without ramifications.

By taking small steps, matching projects with talent, setting the example, staying methodical, and encouraging individual responsibility, you will eventually become comfortable when delegating. With practice, delegating will become one of your most powerful, productive tools—and a ticket out of the standard workplace meeting.

KNOW THE FIRST PARADOX OF DELEGATING

The First Paradox of Delegating is that delegating almost always means more control, not less, when it is properly carried out.

As mentioned before, one of the fears associated with delegating is the concern that handing over responsibility means relinquishing control. No need to fear: the interesting irony about delegating is that it invariably means more hands-on control for managers. Here's why.

First, skillful delegating takes planning. It means creating a list of projects you would like to delegate and charting the course for each of them. It means scheduling one-on-one time with each worker to assign each project and, later, to review that worker's progress and performance. It means keeping track of projects and knowing at any given time the person in charge of a task. It means knowing the strengths and weaknesses of individuals on your team and the ongoing improvement of those with weaknesses.

Planning means being involved. And an involved manager is a hands-on manager.

Another reason delegating means hands-on management is that, since more people are completing the tasks at hand, more work can be added. Therefore, more work is getting done—both by your team and by you. Again, each minute of time you spend properly delegating produces four minutes of time for yourself. The key is to force yourself to make that initial time investment.

Delegating also translates into hands-on management because of an interesting concept I call the Coaching Effect. In short, a manager becomes more knowledgeable about a task once it has been assigned to another person, just as, say, a football player becomes more knowledgeable about football once he makes the transition to coach.

In the Army, I remember having to research powerful cannon gunpowder that no one in our unit had ever fired with before. Knowing that I would have to hand control of this propellant over to my soldiers, I became a quick expert on how to handle these charges and make use of them.

My soldiers could sense my engrossment. "Hey, sir," they teased, "why don't you come on over and fire one?"

I had been hoping they would ask! I positioned myself properly at the cannon, pulled the lanyard, and fired a charge so powerful it forced the breech nearly into the ground.

If it weren't for delegating the control and use of this gunpowder over to others, I doubt if I would have been as curious about the propellant. The Coaching Effect suggests that the more we delegate, the more we take interest in the tasks that have been handed out.

Since delegating does not involve meetings, there is inherently more *face time* and focus time. Delegating by its design means more valuable management feedback. It is very easy for us to cocoon ourselves in our own personal, daily tasks, rituals, and worries. Perhaps delegating is the force-feeding we need to get ourselves directly into the paths of those we're responsible for. Rather than holding meetings and *pretending* we're involved with the people present and the issues covered, delegating puts us on the front line, encountering those people and issues in a very personal, effective way. Says marketing expert Erik Skaggs: "Delegating changes managing from a distant, top-down process to a personal, bottom-up endeavor. After delegating tasks, you get individual feedback on each task's success. The more successes there are, the more likely you will turn them into patterns for broader management strategies."

Again, the wonderful paradox of delegation is that, while you're turning over important tasks and projects to others, you're placing yourself directly where the action is. Delegating means anything but losing touch. The manager who delegates is *the* quintessential hands-on manager. If you shrink from delegating, for any of the reasons mentioned, you fail to fully realize the time and productivity potential that exists when you task out of your obligations and responsibilities.

KNOW THE SECOND PARADOX OF DELEGATING

The Second Paradox of Delegating is that delegating does not diminish but rather enhances your standing as a leader, when it is properly carried out.

It doesn't take long to find managers who believe that they're questioning their own leadership by delegating. I have watched many a team leader afraid to relinquish even the most mundane of tasks.

With cyclical downsizing being a part of today's normal business strategies, job preservation might have something to do with a manager's hesitation to delegate. I remember starting with a new company as a department shift supervisor, where I was distressed to find that, whenever a supervisor took vacation, the two other shift supervisors simply closed the gap left by the vacationing boss, each working a 12-hour shift. In essence, no one really was legitimately getting time off—they were just swapping hours in the long run.

"Hey," I finally asked a group of my contemporaries, with the wide eyes of an innocent child, "why don't we train some people to take our places as supervisors, so that we can take some real vacation time?"

"For heaven's sake, don't say that too loudly!" pleaded one of the other supervisors—looking around to see if anyone else was in earshot. "The last thing we need around here is other people learning our jobs."

"But why?"

"If they can do without you for a day, they can do without you forever."

Whew! *That's* paranoia. But the underlying question is fair enough: if you enable people around you to complete many of your assignments, aren't you delegating yourself out of a job? Aren't you, in essence, becoming less of a leader?

My experience suggests just the opposite. I've had a colleague say to me, "As long as I'm the only one who knows how to do this, they can *never* let me go"—only to be shown the door a few weeks later by upper management.

Delegating, in a sense, means training, and I have found that the managers who develop reputations as being the best trainers are very often those people an organization considers the most valuable. They're visible, knowledgeable, and willing to share their experiences. That's not to say good people don't get let go for dumb reasons. Sometimes they do. (Maybe their fate was determined at a flawed meeting!) But to the extent that an organization carries out judicious decision making in deciding who is important to the group, the involved, proficient delegator is hardly considered dead wood.

Packaging and shipping supervisor John Decker agrees. "I used to feel the need to be involved in everything," he admits. "But now, I'm very comfortable with training and delegating most things. Yeah, it may look like I'm managing myself out of a job—but my company knows that I'm just freeing myself up to move on to another set of priorities."

On a subliminal level, organizations tend to view people who delegate as strong leaders rather than people trying to pass off their work. And rightfully so. Delegating *is* leadership. The process of delegating forces you—in a good way—to get to know your people and appropriately use their individual talents.

Knowing each person's unique abilities and limitations will help you to assign them to the tasks that suit them best. As asked before, isn't it probable that each person where you work can do *one* thing better than you? Why not allow your entire team to outperform you—one person and one task at a time? If the end result is better team performance (of which you'll certainly share the credit), why not assign responsibility in such a way that you're outperformed each and every day and way?

The point is not to blend delegating with leadership, as if delegating were the awful vegetables you mixed with your mash potatoes as a kid to help them go down. The point is to make delegating such an effective tool that your team will look better and you'll have more time to accomplish things. Delegating becomes a tool of leadership—not a competitor with it.

Furthermore, getting to know your team through delegating can take you to another dimension of positive involvement. Handing them work means getting involved. It means asking someone "*How are you doing?*" as more than simply a greeting—and standing there for a while as a worker elaborates on a problem. Such involvement allows you a peek into that worker's personal life. It's not prying if it's offered voluntarily and without prodding questions. And it offers you a different take on your people than simply what they do for a living.

For example, I remember once striking up a conversation with an older gentleman who filled a basic machine operator's job at my plant, operating a slow, somewhat outdated piece of machinery. To the casual observer, this man might have seemed as outmoded as the machine itself. After talking with him, however, I learned that his life was rich with knowledge about production and management. He held a university degree earned in Poland. He had gotten his education during the years of Soviet influence. I was stunned to learn that, as a student, he had been forced to learn the Russian language. As it turned out, his understanding of Russian gave him the opportunity to manage Russian immigrants when he first arrived at the United States. After learning more about him, I found myself considering his technical expertise and his management advice a lot more seriously. It was useful wisdom I never would have been exposed to had I not stopped for a while to learn more about a worker.

Gathering such knowledge is more than just being a good guy: if you take a personal interest in the success of others as you delegate, you'll find your investment coming back to you tenfold.

That's the Second Paradox of Delegating. Delegating doesn't contradict leadership; it's leadership in action.

RECOGNIZE WHEN RESPONSIBILITY IS NO LONGER A REWARD

I am a firm believer that delegating is a form of flattery and that if you hand out responsibility as if it were a reward, people will consider it as such. Nothing makes a person feel better than when people in charge say, "Hey, we think you can handle this." I also go further by saying that productive, dependable workers possess a deep-down desire for additional responsibility—whether they want to admit it or not.

However, when executing this "responsibility as reward" philosophy, keep in mind that it has its important limitations. I sometimes watch in amazement how an endless amount of work gets dumped on a few, highly competent people who stand out in an organization. Sometimes they resist. Other times, they leave the organization—much to the surprise of the people who've been doing the dumping.

At some point, the reward of additional responsibility begins to lose its charm.

Numerous professional journals have published studies that put analytical substance to what should be obvious: people cannot be handed an endless amount of additional work without a diminishing return on the payroll cost savings. Even if additional money is offered along with the additional work, once people feel exploited (rather than simply depended upon), they go through periods of bitter feelings and reduced productivity.

The condition of good people going sour often results from laziness or inattention on the part of the supervisor. It's easier to flood the best people with all the work than to spend time coaching, mentoring, or counseling the average people who need feedback to do better. You need to make it a point—no matter how much time and effort it takes—to delegate assignments even to the most lazy, incapable, or apprehensive people who surround you, and to follow through on monitoring their progress. At the very least, you will have started work files on people who, well, need to have files started on them. At most, you will see a return on your invested time when some of those people get better at performing assigned tasks, perhaps perceiving their greater responsibility the way it should be perceived and becoming better employees in general. Also, you will have made it known to all of your workers that they are fairly sharing the work at hand and that good work does not simply reap *more* work.

Avoid working the good horse to death. If someone does a great job for you, don't react by pouring it on. You'll hurt yourself by becoming overly reliant on this person, resulting in a disproportionate amount of delegated work. You'll hurt the team by making this person disheartened, disgruntled, or just plain burnt out. I have seen wonderful employees transformed into nonperforming, marble likenesses by an unfair saturation of work assignments. It's no wonder that some people live by the *never volunteer for anything* creed. If the reward for good performance is work overload, then what's the point of judiciously carrying out delegated work?

Ensure that the people on your team are assigned their fair shares of work. Enthusiastic, high performers should be remunerated with more important, high-visibility assignments (that, again, should be presented and perceived as rewards). If you have the authority to give an assignment that has some degree of gratification, such as a business trip or an overnight training visit to a nice area, do so. On the other end of the spectrum, poor performers should be greeted with more work along the same, or lower, level of importance, with your coaching—or even your written counseling—along the way.

Unfortunately, most good people will not tell you when they're overloaded. Mind reading is not part of management job descriptions, but it should be. You need to sense when an employee perceives an assignment as a sign of faith and when it is viewed as an unwanted burden.

Also remember that *some* burden and discomfort is a good thing—such as the pain you feel after a good workout. Handing people tasks past the point of comfort can be a necessary way of making them better thinkers and, eventually, good managers. "People need to be taught how to juggle many balls," says Special Ops major Ron Green. "No one wants a team player who only can juggle one glass ball."

So what is that magic, optimum point where a person receives the most positive reinforcement from additional responsibility without approaching overload? That's a tough call. It probably exists in a relative state of stability in the workplace—which means it is best to gauge the steadiness of your surroundings before setting your level of delegating. In today's environment of periodic downsizing and cross training, the venue for successful project assigning can easily be disturbed. For example, if layoffs have occurred recently, delegate only to the point where you even out the newly unassigned responsibilities—and let things settle down before utilizing delegating any further. Make sure you are familiar with the workloads of those around you before assigning multiple tasks.

Regardless of the situation, never lose sight of what it is you're trying to do: reward others with added responsibility, relieve yourself of some projects and tasks, and establish yourself as that unique manager who can hand out and monitor assignments without the useless vehicle of a staff meeting.

SUMMARY

- Managers who fear delegating often try to compensate by holding meetings.

- Managers should practice delegating by taking small steps at first, concentrating on projects over routine duties, setting the example, matching skills to tasks, staying organized, and encouraging individual responsibilities.

- Rather than relinquishing control, the manager who delegates invariably gains more hands-on control.

- Delegating does not diminish the manager's standing as a leader. Delegating enhances it.

- Handing out responsibility can be treated as and perceived as a reward—but only up to a point.

CHAPTER 7

Use Technology When Possible

GET OUT OF REAL TIME

Is it possible to create 200 productive hours each day by replacing just *one* meeting with a little technology? That's what Dave Ebbrecht did. He's the general director of Kansas City Southern Railroad's transportation coordination center in Shreveport, Louisiana. At one point, the railroad's 100 field managers were spending over two hours each morning, every morning, on a telephone conference call. Ebbrecht recognized this inefficient meeting method for exchanging railroad scheduling information. "It was a nightmare," he says. "The same details were being repeated again and again as different people joined in on the call." Subsequently, he designed and implemented a shared, computer network spreadsheet, accessible to all field managers and yard managers in a dozen states. The telephone meetings no longer take place. And 200 hours of productive management time are freed each day from the shackles of a monster conference call.

Ebbrecht says that, once liberated from this daily ritual, managers immediately began taking advantage of their newfound time. "It had gotten to where you had a group of communicators and a group of executors. Without those conference calls, now everyone is an executor."

What can technology do for you to replace meetings and free up your day? The most beneficial timesaving aspect of technology is that it takes you out of *real time*. As mentioned earlier, the sharing of real time is the worst characteristic of any meeting. People have to block out large parts of their daily schedules in order to communicate simultaneously in a group.

Curiously, it's the real-time property of meetings that *attract* so many people to its use. When a meeting is being held, managers have the false comfort of thinking that the minute they are saying something, it is getting heard and absorbed. If they seek feedback, it can be instantaneous. Many managers equate meeting time with *face time*, as there is something reassuring when they see all the faces of a group in one room at one time—providing the illusion that everyone is on the same sheet of music.

We know, of course, that such presumptions are folly. The productive manager is one that garners input and disseminates output outside of real time. As such, you must be open to—and eventually dependent upon—nonmeeting ways to communicate with workers, managers, and others involved with projects and the day-to-day administration of those around you. Technology is the key.

We've covered the advantages of one-on-one management. Technology supports the one-on-one encounter more than anything else does. An electronic burst of information is a laser beam of urgency aimed directly at your team member (or pointed by your team member directly at you). An electronic burst of information cannot be interrupted by side topics, obstructions, or the personal agendas of others—and cannot be altered by the filtering effect of groupthink. If you desire 10 different takes on the same issue, then sending out 10 separate bursts soliciting such input makes all the sense in the world. The returned data will be unique, enlightening, and undiluted.

One-on-one communication becomes much more efficient when it's pulled out of real time.

Along with requests for opinion, the one-on-one technological encounter is also ideal for disseminating raw information and work direction. There is very little distraction when a team member is given news or assignments from a message that can be screened more than once. The encounter allows for questions, clarifications, and response. When the team member is finished digesting the information, there should be little confusion over what's happening or what's expected.

SEE WHAT TECHNOLOGIES ARE AVAILABLE

Bruce Backa is the founder and CEO of NTP Software, a company that develops business software and provides computer network storage management. Backa makes no bones about his antimeeting philosophy. Says one of his technical officers: "Bruce manages more people directly than the business books say is possible, and yet he has a *very* nonmeeting leadership style."

Backa sees technology helping the meetingless manager in two ways. First, virtual work environments are allowing people to work farther and farther apart, making overblown staff meetings less geographically practicable. Second, as technology brings about a wider variety of mechanisms for communicating, more and more people are finding modes that they're comfortable with.

You should always take an interest in new venues of communication. The time-conscious manager should examine current communications and information technologies as well as take a second look at some not-so-current technologies. Your emphases should be on the gathering and disseminating of information rather than on the bells and whistles of the gizmos themselves.

As you wean yourself of your appetite for meetings, you'll find an endless supply of technological alternatives. Following an *everything in moderation* philosophy (i.e., not going overboard), you can embrace technology in such a way as to facilitate an exchange of ideas and sustain your time management. Today's opportunities along these regards seem almost revolutionary, as advances in communication appear to be progressing exponentially. View the possibilities presented by these improvements the same way a colonial letter scribe might have viewed the possibilities of the telephone. As modes of transmitting evolve in ways we are only beginning to imagine, the notion of immediate access to anyone for any reason gains substance. Is this an exaggeration? Maybe so, but consider that, as recently as the early 1990s, the concept of fully interactive television was the stuff of science fiction. As each day passes, electronic communication becomes quicker, cleaner, more detailed and, most importantly, more interactive.

The current technologies include hybrids of pagers, wireless telephones, and modems for accessing the Internet and the World Wide Web. These mobile Web combinations allow you to obtain immediate information on any number of topics, much of which can keep decision-making techniques very dynamic and enhanced. With such devices, you can send and retrieve e-mail or cyber-chat with a group member—or several group members at once (not that you would *want* to). You can summon someone to submit feedback or call the office. Or *you* can be summoned. This information can be catalogued and filed for later retrieval—all with a quick paging, scanning, and clicking of the control. Again, consider how far this technology has come in such a short time. How long ago was the idea of reaching into a purse or pocket and speaking to someone an outlandish idea? How long ago was the dream of having instantaneous access to unlimited data far-fetched? At present, it is all very accessible with the press of a button, making immediate the obtaining of knowledge, the dissemination of directives, and the acquiring of input from others. These are truly wonderful, astonishing times!

Curiously, what is getting the most attention at this writing? Text messaging—short, to the point written messages that are sent to mobile handsets within seconds of transmission. They save time because they don't require accessing, and managers can tailor them as *alerts*—where people plan scheduled messages to serve as appointment and task reminders. "Text messages are great," says Karen Barry, a district manager for Verizon Wireless. "They're quick, concise, and discreet— which means you won't be interrupting anyone if you read them in a meeting." In a meeting? Hmmm. Perhaps something *is* getting accomplished in some staff meetings these days, as a dozen individuals in one room secretly manage their teams via silent, mobile transmitters.

Text messaging is noteworthy in that, even though the messages are instantaneous, the interaction still occurs outside of real time. The manager is not obliged to respond immediately and, therefore, is not distracted from the activity at hand. A second benefit: the messages are inherently brief and pertinent—just the way a true leader likes them.

Such technology not only simplifies communication between a group and its leader, but also it advances a new type of group, a *cybergroup*, as a viable team structure that does not affront the philosophies of meetingless management and organizational channeling. Quite the opposite: virtual teams via the Web *celebrate* the individual and individual contribution. Group members need not be geographically nearby. Furthermore, group membership can be ever-changing based on the needs and goals of the leader.

In 1998, management authors Kimball Fisher and Mareen Duncan Fisher suggested the idea of far-reaching *virtual knowledge teams.*

Interestingly, they admitted to not being sure if technology was meeting needs or creating new needs. In other words, they suggested that perhaps virtual teams were being created because of the technology rather than the initial need. In either case, they found the end result the same: people meeting without *meeting*. Fisher and Fisher regarded the concept of virtual teaming as very liberating. A personal example: while writing their book, *The Distributed Mind*, they did not meet their researcher, Lucas Birdeau, for an entire year!

One thing is for certain: the less physically constrictive a group is, the more assorted and varied its membership—and therefore its diversity of ideas—becomes. Remember the six blind men and the elephant? How about 1000 people studying an elephant from their individual perspectives via the Web? How many different purposes could *they* come up with for that elephant?

When embracing such communication advances, it is probably worth doing so with a marked degree of constraint. Be wary of too much technology or of spending too much time tending to it. Technology for its own sake might be suffocating—and it might turn off the people around you. Whether technological advances display a new need, or whether a need creates the catalyst for technological change, the common thread is the *need*. It must exist. As techo-financial analysts continue to ponder the crash of high-tech stocks and the failures of hundreds of large dot-com companies at the start of this millennium, their inquiries ultimately will rest on the age-old sales concept: if there is no need (or perceived need), there is no sale. Similarly, forcing your group to communicate with the latest technological gadgetry without clarifying the need will make them less enthusiastic about using it. Also, make sure *you* are convinced of these benefits, as you will be the one to persuade others about the merits of learning something new.

As you create methods for people to either contact you or deposit their input for later consideration, you make yourself more accessible than you ever were when meetings controlled your day. Via electronic communication, you open up your schedule to inquest, influence, and inspiration.

There's little point in expanding on the latest communication and information technologies. By the time you read this book, such systems and devices will either be passé or in transition. That's how fast things are moving. There are, however, ways for you to review what's available and to determine what's best for staying in touch with your team.

How quickly can it get a report to you?

Nothing keeps the need for meetings at bay more than receiving daily reports from your team members. They should be VERY brief so as not to become a burdensome chore. (Half a written page at most.) They provide a valuable way to learn about the progression of group projects, the success or failures of work activities, employee questions and concerns, and the seeking of advice. I remember having to maintain a daily log as a shift manager. This simple journal—which eventually was entered and accessed on a computer network shared file—became a very helpful source of information for our senior managers. Urgent questions were brought up. Important innovations were documented. Proper machine settings were recorded. New product trials were chronicled.

In turn, senior managers responded on this shared electronic log—and their influence extended past the normal business hours of operation.

Choose technology that keeps such reports easy to produce, transfer, and access.

Does it keep you inquisitive?

Effective leaders do not have ON-OFF switches. The observant and inquisitive leader works outside the framework of a schedule and a physical environment. The proficient group leader is always ON, is often available, and sees enough outside the confines of an office to ask questions or seek clarifications. A good leader is always "watching," in a sense, and always wants to know more.

Choose technology that makes information and people very accessible and that keeps loads of information close at hand.

Is it compatible with systems outside your team?

Transportation director Dave Ebbrecht suggests that the best communication extends outside the confines of your team or company. "Why is e-mail such a powerful tool?" he asks rhetorically. "It's because e-mail is universal—and very effective for planning and coordinating with organizations outside your company." He's right. There's not a lot of sense in having the latest and greatest of anything if you're limiting your points of contact.

Is it really necessary?

Again, if there's no need for it, think twice about using it. For example, if your team works in the same physical location and you can publicize something on a good, old-fashioned announcement board, then perhaps an electronic shared file isn't necessary.

As you consider what technology is available, take into account the level of computer/technical literacy of those around you. If you post an electronic discussion page, for example, you want it set up so that everyone wishes to log on, read it, and perhaps contribute thoughts to it.

LEARN TO LOVE E-MAIL AND VOICE MAIL

Now that you've considered the new technologies, why not reconsider and celebrate some of the old ones?

E-mail is, in my mind, the most understated human interaction advancement in recent history. It has created an entire culture of on-the-spot announcements and assertions, not to mention an insurgency of mass mailings, chain letters, misinformation, and urban legends. It even has created a new workplace personality—*the e-mail aggressor*, someone who writes and sends scathing e-mail messages but displays meek behavior when confronted face-to-face about them. More importantly, e-mail has brought using the written word for expression back into the mainstream. Letter writing is back! And its transmission is now instantaneous. Good thing, too, as written messages can carry infinitely more detailed and understandable information than a spoken communiqué. Today it is commonplace to send multipaged corporate reports or engineering schematics to large numbers of people for their review, with little effort. For the leader, the advantage is being able to contact every member of the group, provide and solicit lots of information, and have every member respond—without even one face-time or real-time contact. E-mail's strong suit is that people can examine and access data at their own different paces and thoughtfully prepare their individual feedback. Its influence on communication and management has been revolutionary.

NTP Software's Bruce Backa hails the *non-real-time* feature of e-mail. "E-mail reflects the most insightful thoughts of people," he says, "because as soon as you think of something important or imaginative, you can jot it down and send it off electronically. By the time a meeting rolls around or you see the person the idea pertains to, the thought might otherwise be gone from your mind."

Backa foresees a new generation of e-mail on the horizon—"e-mail with intelligence" is what he calls it. Such e-mail essentially will self-determine where it is supposed to go and in what format. "All of today's communication pieces don't quite fit together yet," he observes. "I believe the picture will be complete when the messages we send out can think for themselves, reflecting our intentions and communication goals."

Voice mail is another older technology that bears a second look. Now, what nice things can you say about voice mail without starting a barroom brawl? It seems that bosses and workers universally despise it—possibly more than they despise smiley-face notepads. This distaste is unfortunate because properly used voice mail is the perfect example of an alternative method for dispersing and gathering information. Not only does voice mail allow the trading of information without real-time interface, but the recording of one's voice can provide inflection and urgency that might not otherwise get conveyed. Voice mail is, in many ways, the closest thing to conversation without face-to-face discussion.

So why the bad rap? Why is voice mail loathed so much by so many? There are two probable causes. First, a recorded message is the first thing people hear when the person they are trying to contact by phone is not around. Rather than an opportunity to leave a message, voice mail is seen (sometimes appropriately) as a roadblock to getting in touch with someone. Second, since voice mail was one of the first replacements for real-time interaction, it holds an old, impersonal repute that it may never overcome. Granted, there is something repellent about hearing a recorded message asking for another recorded message. And there is something manifestly distant about hearing a recording of someone's voice rather than hearing the person speak in the here and now. But given its advantage for exchanging information without physical or real-time contact, voice mail should be a valuable tool in any manager's box of memo-bearing tricks.

Your ongoing mission is to strike the right balance between new and old modes of communication, without ever feeling too comfortable to lock a group into a rut. Mix it up and keep the process of corresponding vigorous—even fun!

TRY COMBINING TECHNOLOGIES

A great leader is a dynamic leader, always trying different ways of getting the job done and interested in that one new thing that might push her team to greater achievements. In similar fashion, you should be willing to experiment with and combine an assortment of technologies, perhaps even using different modes with different parts of your team. Bruce Backa refers to these combinations as "creative paradigms." Keep the communications process from growing stale. Add an edge to it, and keep it thriving.

My favorite low-tech combination is voice mail with a pager link. This is a wireless service that alerts your pager whenever someone leaves a message on your voice mail. With this option, you have immediate knowledge of someone trying to contact you without the real-time obligation of having to respond.

I also like the pager/wireless phone combination as well, where you give out your pager number rather than your wireless phone number. Again, you know immediately who is trying to call (and, in the case of advanced pagers, you have a detailed message about why they're calling). But since *you* control the wireless phone, you're not automatically sucked into real time. The decision to contact that person immediately or whenever convenient is yours.

Sometimes one form of communication can work well as an undercurrent against another form. I compare this combination to passing written notes to someone during class. While the main interaction is between the teacher and the students, the riptide is the passing of notes. Hopefully, the notes are a comment on the subject matter— and not just love letters! Another example is how, during a large, useless teleconference, individuals at different facilities might e-mail each other and comment one-on-one about what is being discussed at large. The teleconference itself is defective management, but the notion of people basically communicating on two different tiers is the type of spiritedness that defines good organizational interaction.

I suggest that a two-tiered system is much more effective when it combines two types of broadcasts outside of real time. The first might be spam e-mail, informing the team of a new project or new objectives. The second tier might then be individual voice mails soliciting personal opinions, and then perhaps a discussion page on the Web or the organization's intranet, asking for threads of group comment—available for all to read and respond to.

Having taken many accredited graduate courses online, I think their most exhilarating aspect is the combination of ways the professor coordinates the class. There are computer e-mails, online real-time discussions, threads of discussion that are contributed to over long periods of time (and are therefore out of real time), voice mails, phone calls—even FedEx! As many of these topics carry through the duration of the course, and since they involve so many different ways of conversing, I think they're often more stimulating than traditional classroom education.

Keep your team's information flow from growing stagnant. Combine your assets and keep things lively.

BEWARE OF THE PITFALLS OF ALTERNATIVE COMMUNICATION

As you embrace a particular technology or combination of technologies, be sure to understand and compensate for their drawbacks and liabilities.

One drawback is cost. If the money you're pouring into a communications system cannot be justified by the productivity you're going to get out of it, you might want to look elsewhere. Or you may want to wait until the device is no longer the latest and greatest thing. The cost of most technology drops dramatically once it becomes the *second* latest and greatest thing. If the status of having the fastest processor or the tiniest wireless telephone is important to you or the image of your organization, then weigh the value of that status against the price of the newest gadget.

One hazard of any new technology is its learning curve—and some curves are steeper than others are. Everyone fears the unknown, and some people are downright terrified of new electronic accessories. How many people do you know still have a VCR because they're apprehensive about DVD players? And out of those, how many still have flashing zeroes on their VCR because they're apprehensive about learning to set the time? And out of those, how many have black tape over the flashing zeroes because they're apprehensive and annoyed about the flashing? People take time to learn and get comfortable with new things. But if the time invested into getting your team trained up on a new system doesn't match or exceed the time and productivity benefits, then you might want to reconsider taking the plunge.

Another problem with technology is that not everyone might be as excited about getting out of real time as you are. People may not understand that the grand purpose of these alternative technologies is to keep them where they function the best without losing touch. They also may be nervous about leaving written or verbal messages without the gratification of an immediate response. In this sense, technology is a bit of a paradox: it creates faster communication but removes the obligation of immediate retrieval or response. Your team needs to be sold on the idea that while communication should be timely, it need not pull them away from a task at hand (and into a meeting, for example). Admittedly, this important philosophy may not be convincing even to some managers, much less to their teams. But people ultimately must be won over on the impression of fast delivery of information without the indulgence of an immediate answer.

Another drawback to communication technology is its impersonal nature. No matter how inefficient it may be, any contact involving a "real" person, a human voice, or a sympathetic ear is going to be preferable to more practical but less personal ways of relating information. Why, so many years after their contrivance, are singing telegrams still popular? Is it the personalized nature of the message? Is it the embarrassed look of the recipient (perhaps receiving the message amongst an office crowd)? Or is it the buzz one gets being in the presence of this flesh-and-bone transmittal, singing and performing, all for one person? It may seem unrefined for some, but one thing is certain: a singing telegram is seldom forgotten.

So how do you take advantage of the time and efficiency benefits of alternative communication while maintaining an aura of sociability and inclusion, or at least without generating a dramatically impersonal setting for expression? Again, try mixing it up. If you incorporate several different modes of communication, then you increase your likelihood of passing along information effectively and maintaining a positive influence over the group. Your combinations should be lively and adaptable as you experiment with different blends for getting a point across. For example, you might send e-mail soliciting progress reports from several departments. Once responding e-mail messages are received, you might then call the department heads to ask follow-up questions on the reports. Or you might "chat" on-line with members of a cyber-team, and follow up with voice mail messages to those members who need special direction or have tasks meriting special reflection.

Make sure you emphasize the freedom these new technologies will bring. That is, if you are freeing people from meetings and making yourself more open and accessible through these accessories, let the people know it. At some point, their appreciation for the extra time, the efficient communication, and your refined aura of openness and approachability may offset the perception of detachment.

As you employ communication technologies, be wary of their filtering effects. Absolute communication involves all the senses. A total intercommunication example is eating at a restaurant. The patronizing couple looks at the menu. They smell the distinctive cuisine the restaurant is known for. They hear the dinner music as the waiter recites the specials of the day. Then they might touch each other's hand while tasting a glass of wine before the meal. Dining is the ultimate communication experience. Taking away any of these sensory portals, or diminishing them somehow, lessens the experience. Such is the filtering effect of some alternative communication modes. For example, any type of transmission that is not face-to-face might filter the sound of gravity in a person's voice or the look of enthusiasm on his face. As with an electronic birthday greeting sent to one's computer instead of a singing telegram sent to one's office, the "buzz" is gone. Moreover, if this filtering effect is passed from team member to team member, it may diminish or dissolve the point of the initial message. One thinks back to *Wonderama*, the Saturday kids' show of the 1960s and early 1970s, where Bob McAllister asked children, one at a time, to relay a sentence from one child to the next. As each child was brought out to hear the sentence echoed, the utterance was mutated ever so slightly. Collectively, by the time the statement made its way through 10 children, the original sentence was ravished. Such is the potential shortcoming of alternative communication.

The solution is a leader willing to follow a message through several means and generations of transmission. There is nothing wrong with periodically asking your team members whether or not messages are received and interpreted in a manner consistent with their original intent. A way to augment this technique, again, is to employ an assorted and vigorous combination of communication tactics. You should send your communication in a manner that keeps people interested, informed, and able to follow up on earlier communicated data and directives.

As you employ new means for communicating, you might have to offset concerns that the new technology makes you too much the center of attention, as if you are the clearinghouse for all information and decision making. To be sure, the concepts of meetingless management and organizational channeling are built on the belief that the leader is THE center of focus in any establishment—and, therefore, must ultimately call the shots. However, these doctrines do not rely solely on the actions of the leader and they do not reject participative management. In fact, the ultimate goal of organizational channeling is to embrace the ideals behind participative management—only without surrendering to some of the debilitating structures it has created over the years. Much of the process involves the gathering of membership input and monitoring membership actions—both steps refuting the idea that the leader is the only one doing anything or contributing to decisions. Make sure your technology does not create a dark curtain over the cooperative and synergetic outlook you're trying to create amongst your team.

Also, make sure that your technology doesn't pigeonhole your team members to the point that their perspectives are too narrowed. Granted, organizational channeling does not require everyone to see the big picture at once. Everyone should have their talents working towards their own part of this picture. However, the big picture should never be hidden or held back in a selfish way. You should always describe your preeminent objectives to your group, and you should work to keep all group members informed of the group's progress. Channeling means keeping people aware of the big picture without having to dwell on it ad nauseam, and without distracting them with all of the *little* pictures other than their own.

To the extent that technology can sometimes seem impersonal, you need to ensure that it does not distort channeling into feelings of isolation. Feeling left out could be mostly perception, but it can be a damaging perception and one that you must work to resist.

Along these same lines, don't allow technology to make team communicating seem secretive in nature. You don't want technology to create a perception of power through concealed knowledge. Yes, organizational channeling is built on the idea of diverting varied attention, information, and energy to specific individuals for the sake of tapping into their unique talents. And this method does not advocate sharing every aspect of a plan and every conduit of channeling with everyone. However, such restraint on your part should not turn into outright concealment. And secrets should never be squirreled away—to be revealed later in bits and pieces to forge interest or support among the group.

Again, perceptions can be equally detrimental to a team as reality. In the instance of secrecy, perception may actually *lead* to reality, as people perceiving secretiveness around them might, in turn, keep their own cards close to their vests. And so, whether justified or not, the perception of secrecy must be avoided and—if it arises—squelched.

Don't allow technology to exacerbate fears of secret subgroups and hidden agendas.

Remember that the point of improved technology is to create a working atmosphere of shared knowledge and accessibility. Your openness and forthrightness in handing out tasks could go a long way in allaying fears of secrecy. The key is one of approachability, of unwavering integrity on your part, and of your insistence that such candor be emulated throughout the group.

Make certain that your technology doesn't neutralize the time benefits you're trying to get out of it. Some new technology might be too time-consuming or just plain defective—where you wind up spending an undue amount of your time reading manuals, calling technicians, and chasing down customer service people. Perhaps the best way to avoid such a trap is to employ new technology incrementally. Instead of outfitting your entire organization with new mobile Web devices, why not purchase just two of them? Keep one and pass along one to an important team member. You might even consider giving it to the person on your team *least* likely to embrace new technology. As the weeks progress, see how you two communicate. Is it fast and efficient, or does the process slow you down? Are there too many bugs in the software or hardware? Monitor and track your results. If the time spent implementing and utilizing this new gadget is less than the time spent conducting business as usual, then—from a time management perspective—the equipment is justified.

The common thread to challenging these negative aspects of alternative communication is a leader who ultimately wants to celebrate and utilize the unique qualities in each individual—not stifle them. Once communication turns oppressive, secretive, or time-consuming, the process becomes an aberration. You must remain ever proactive in keeping your management methods true to form, and to reap the rewards of avoiding meetings and freeing up people's time. Let technology be your ticket to more time and more hands-on control.

SUMMARY

- Communication and information technologies are important tools for gathering feedback and providing supervision outside of real time. Managers should be open to nonmeeting, technological ways of communicating within their own world and the world around them.

- Managers always should take an interest in new venues of communication. When considering a new technology, they should look at its speed, compatibility, and necessity.

- E-mail and voice mail are wonderful ways of communicating outside of real time.

- The best means of communicating is probably a combination of several technologies.

- Managers should be wary of the pitfalls of alternative communication, including cost, information distortion, resistance to change, perceptions of impersonal correspondence, and perceptions of secrecy.

CHAPTER 8

Get a Mentor, Be a Mentor

DISCOVER THE CONCEPT OF MENTORING

Why has the notion of mentoring fallen out of favor? Does anyone know what it is anymore?

Mentoring is little more than taking someone under your wing with the hope of providing guidance and early career development. It begins with seeing a new employee at work who reminds you of yourself as a young worker or young manager. This new person may or may not work directly for you—although I would suggest that the best mentoring occurs when you mentor someone that you directly manage. Without openly exhibiting partiality towards this person, you take an interest to the point of offering career-building advice, perhaps sharing a trade secret or two along the way. You remain approachable and willing to listen as this person comes to you with problems and seeks counsel. You monitor this person's progress throughout the months, even years, putting in a good word to the right decision makers when promotions are being considered. And as this person eventually leaves your direct influence for another department or another office—or even another company—and as this person reaches professional heights that are perhaps much higher than your own achievements or accomplishments, you can take stock in the fact that you had something to do with someone else's success. From a personal sense of worth, mentoring is a nice way to ensure that—in light of constantly changing corporate strategies and management philosophies and social norms—you can still take some of the old, hard, consistent lessons you have learned in life and pass them on to another generation of achievers.

"Mentoring is sharing some of the dimensions of leadership that fall outside of training classes and trends," says regional business manager Karen Barry. "When mentored, people learn ideals like practicing etiquette, tracking career paths, proper interviewing, promoting solutions, and setting a good example."

You would think that young workers might acknowledge their naiveté and eagerly embrace the offerings of a mentor. They don't. Many people new to a job enter their situations convinced they have all the answers. I recently saw a sign posted in a restaurant. It said, "Hire a teenager—while he still knows everything!" Such an attitude endures into one's younger employment years.

In many ways, we encourage the lack of interest in mentoring. Corporate culture today tends to glorify the young know-it-all. Youthfulness and fresh ideas get preference over dues paid and wisdom learned. And when companies purge their payrolls to cut expenses, they tend to push out the older people, hoping to free up bigger income and benefit costs. The unfortunate side effect is that the experience and knowledge of seasoned team members are devalued as well.

So what are we left with? If organizations feel comfortable seeking young people with all the answers, and if new employees enter a group without formal or informal coaching from experienced members, where do they turn? I suggest that new managers—many of them young and expected to produce grand, instant results—find themselves with nowhere else to turn but to meetings. They become absorbed in them, trying to tap into a murky experience at their workplace as they attempt to influence the actions of others.

Clearly, a new manager—or perhaps a not-so-new-manager in a new department or starting at a new company—can do much better than calling meetings to gather information and experience. Mentoring is the perfect, alternative solution. Finding a mentor can help you learn the current ways of the organization, its successes and failures, its areas of strength, and its ongoing challenges. Tapping into a mentor can get you started in the right direction and can keep you heading that way for months or even years.

And when you've drawn on your mentor long enough that you've learned the ropes, why not become a mentor yourself? Mentoring will serve you better than meetings in influencing the most useful people on your team and in creating actions and situations to make your team prosperous in the future. Serve as a mentor and get to know your people one-on-one. Select for mentoring those team members whose personal successes might have the most dramatic impact on the overall prosperity of the organization.

In short, you should embrace the concept of mentoring from the view up (as you select your mentor) and the view down (as you select your disciples).

SELECT YOUR MENTOR

Some management tactics work pretty darned well—all the way up to the point where they are noticed by upper management! Then they're often formalized, tampered with, mandated, and despised. Why? Once a process stops falling under the category *innovation* and starts falling under the category *formalization,* it loses its allure and, subsequently, its effectiveness.

Aside from its curious aversion for seasoned talent, the corporate world has invalidated mentoring by, at some point, formalizing it and therefore killing it. In a formal mentoring program, a junior employee is arbitrarily assigned to a senior person. I would compare it to being told whom you had to take to the senior prom. Maybe a bond forms, maybe not. Without a personal chemistry and a set of distinctive reasons for selecting one's mentor (or one's disciple), the relationship is likely to grow distant, and the program inevitably withers.

Does that mean we *formalize* mentoring just by insisting that our team members try it? No. It is altogether appropriate for you to demand that a new member of your team seek out the experience of a senior person. Indeed, a legitimate assignment might be having this new team member report on what was learned. You might say, "In one month, come to me with five important idiosyncrasies you have learned about this organization and five ways a senior person has suggested you deal with them."

However, at that point, the new member should have complete freedom in choosing how to gather the advice and from whom these helpful hints are obtained. Choosing one's mentor should be a very informal and innovative endeavor on the part of the employee.

There's a difference between formalizing *results* (telling the new team member to find a mentor) and formalizing a *process* (choosing a mentor for a new team member). Put simply, formalizing results places a requirement on someone but still encourages personal growth and innovation; formalizing a process just turns people off.

The true spirit of mentoring lies in how mentors and students find each other and how they are creative in passing along and taking in experience-related information.

So, assuming that you belong to an organization with an informal mentoring program—or no program at all—how do you go about finding an effective mentor?

Who's available?

The first important step might be to look at the potential teachers available. A mentor does not have to be your direct supervisor. It could be a senior person not connected directly to your manager. It could be an experienced board member—or even a senior administrator with a clear perspective. In some situations, an effective mentor could be a manager retired from the company or an experienced person who has since moved on but still holds the best interests for the company at heart. If this retired manager still has a little pull within the organization, all the better.

It's possible for a mentor to be at a level or tier *under* that of the manager's, such as the seasoned platoon sergeant who, while strictly subordinate to the new, wet-behind-the-ears lieutenant, still takes the lieutenant under his wings and instructs him on becoming a successful young leader. I have benefited from similar situations in the business community. I learned a lot from a senior machine operator who took me, as a new production manager, aside on many occasions and set me straight on a number of things. He explained peculiarities about the machinery I never would have learned from an operations manual. On a personal level, he told me what he respected about good managers and what he disliked about bad ones. And, when it came time to deal with a problem employee, he discreetly told me how other managers had effectively officiated in similar situations.

Who's the ideal mentor?

Surely the quintessential mentor is the senior manager, perhaps one or two levels up from the person seeking career-related guidance. The mentor does not have to be directly a part of the disciple's chain of authority.

The perfect mentor is friendly, eager to listen, and generally accessible. I would argue that the best mentor is one who sees an earlier version of herself in a new person coming to her for counsel.

A mentor-disciple relationship, when properly experienced, can be a very personal ray of sunshine in the dark, impersonal world of business or organizational management—for both parties.

So choose your mentor—and enjoy the sunshine.

SELECT YOUR DISCIPLES

Along this same line of thinking, it is equally appropriate for you, the experienced manager, to choose the people *you* would like to mentor. Selecting the right disciples—people who stand to contribute the most to your organization—can transform a team in dramatic ways. As with selecting your mentor, the process of selecting your student, your "grasshopper," should be an informal and innovative venture.

Who's interested in your guidance?

So how do you figure out whom to take under your wings? Whose development best benefits the organization? And, on a personal level, how do you select someone that will give *you* the greatest sense of fulfillment. Let's face it—training new people, even if it entails nothing more than passing along old philosophies, can turn tedious in no time if it is not enjoyed and if it does not create a sense of personal worth.

When choosing your disciples, why not first consider those who come to you seeking mentorship? The biggest reason most people do not get what they want out of life, on personal and professional levels, is that they simply do not ask for it. If someone appeals to you for guidance, consider the request on the surface as a desire to exceed. It takes a lot of nerve these days to approach someone looking for answers: again, many of us feel as if we are already expected to *know* all the answers. Furthermore, in this fast-paced world, few people step back from the daily putting out of fires to consider the bigger issues of business success and triumphant organizational leadership. The person who steps forward and says, "Yes, I would like to learn about these bigger things" sets himself apart from others. As both a manager and a college business instructor, I can attest that there is no greater joy for a teacher than to be in the presence of eager learners.

Granted, some requests for mentorship may be superficial—people seeking merely to place themselves in front of influential senior people. But these ulterior motives make themselves apparent soon enough; shallow people have a common tendency to expose their lack of depth. Besides, even if someone is using the premise of mentorship as a means of getting noticed, that is not necessarily a sign of being conniving or overly political. It is possible to curry favor and at the same time learn a thing or two. And if someone is trying to exploit these sessions without the prospect of learning from them, then the process will become tedious for both the instructor and the student, and it will end soon enough.

The more likely scenario is that a person asking to learn *wants* to learn. There's no substitute for enthusiasm. Therefore, you should always strongly consider the request of someone seeking mentorship.

Who stands to gain from your time?

When choosing your disciples, consider the raw skills of the people on your team. After all, there is no sense wanting to sculpt if no marble is available. Who displays young, unrefined talent? Who seems to have strong analytical skills? Who presents herself in a professional manner? Who works well with others? Who has the most to offer the organization initially? And who is most likely to be around long enough to positively impact the organization? Sure, successful people have a tendency to move around these days, but still, one must ask—at least theoretically—"Who is this organization's leader in 20 years?" Who is the future CEO?

Your prospective disciples should be fast, eager learners, displaying a capacity to absorb information, analyze it, and take it to heart. They should be open to criticism, as undefensive as possible. They should be young, vibrant minds ready to draw on your energy and ready to energize.

DISCOVER THE FREEDOM IN STRUCTURE

My third-grade daughter was never a bad kid—only an unfettered spirit. I once gave her very specific instructions to wait inside the house by herself and not answer the phone while I walked to the corner store just down the block for her cold medicine. Upon returning, I found her dancing with a parade baton in bare feet on the wet, front lawn.

"Angel," I asked through gritted teeth, "what did I say to you about leaving the house?"

"Sorry, dad," she said with sweet and innocent sincerity. "But you know, sometimes freedom needs freedom."

"Freedom needs freedom?" I stifled a grin. "Who said *that*?"

She turned around, apparently to see if someone was lurking behind her—someone she could blame for putting words in her mouth. "Uh, I guess I did."

And so, in dealing with this vibrant personality, it was with apprehension that I visited my daughter's third-grade teacher—a stern woman with a reputation for being very demanding in the classroom. She was probably the last teacher on earth who still used spelling lists and rote memorization of multiplication tables. Her weekly itineraries were broken down to the minute. Assigned chores, personal discipline, desk neatness—it was all part of her students' daily routine. How was my daughter, the free spirit, handling this regimentation? I was about to find out during a midyear, parent-teacher conference.

My wife and I had hired a sitter, figuring that the teacher would have a lot to say, and that it was best not to have my daughter around.

The first thing I remember seeing was the High Honors sticker on my daughter's folder—straight *As*. "Mr. and Mrs. Snair, your daughter is doing wonderfully." After noting a few high points and a few areas still needing some work, she commented, almost as an afterthought, "On the discipline side, there really isn't a problem. She's maturing into quite a young lady."

The silence was damning, as my wife and I looked at the report card, and then at each other, with our mouths hanging open.

"Is there something wrong?" the teacher asked.

"No," I responded. "No, not at all. I guess we came here this afternoon expecting, well, something of an earful."

"And why's that?"

I hesitated. Then: "I would imagine you're aware of the reputation you have for being a, well, a structured teacher."

"A reputation well deserved."

Sounding like a real softy for a parent, I stammered, "We weren't sure she was going to do well in such an environment."

My wife nodded. "She does love her freedom."

The teacher smiled. "So I've noticed. Perhaps that's why she's done so well in my class. There's lots of freedom in structure."

Again, more silence, then a bit of small talk, some thanks, and off we went.

"Freedom in structure."

Wow! Just a curious statement from my daughter's third-grade teacher. And yet, I consider it one of the most profound things I've ever heard. As contradictory as it sounds on the surface, upon deeper reflection (and perhaps a few happy hour beers), it makes perfect sense. There *is* freedom in structure. In the case of my daughter, a structured classroom environment overseen by her mentor—that is, the teacher—*freed* her from the distractions that previously had kept her from learning and behaving. Her boundaries were established. She knew exactly what was expected of her and when it was expected. I learned later on that her daily routine also included scheduled writing time and playing time. It was no wonder that the written stories and the creative games she brought home with her were bursting with imagination and artistry. She was *free* to create and to learn.

The teacher's point was well founded. When the mentor clearly defines the parameters for the student, the process is very liberating to the creative mind. Handing most competent workers a rule book is like handing a bulk of clay to a sculptor. It's amazing the things people will come up with in order to stay within a given set of guidelines.

Planning and purchasing director John Pastor suggests, "Structure is like having a map in a minefield. The better the map, the faster a person can go."

The first manufacturing job I ever had was at a paper mill in Oswego, New York. We had a machine that could make a variety of paper products. However, shutting the machine off to change from one product to another was a tedious, time-consuming chore. One day, the senior worker—the machine tender—approached his mentor, my boss, with a novel idea. He suggested modifying the machine to change from one product to another *without shutting the machine off!* My boss agreed it was potentially a time-saving and money-saving idea, and we told him to give it a try. However, there were some guidelines. First, modifying the machine while *in process* had to be done safely. Second, any innovations could not be damaging to the equipment. Third, any alterations had to be completed within 30 minutes. (Making more than 30 minutes' worth of off-grade, substandard paper would have offset the time benefits of keeping the machine running.) Other than those restrictions, my boss's guidance was to go for it!

You know the rest of the story. This worker and his crew grabbed the football and ran with it. After a few trial runs, they were able to change from one similar product to another, with the machine still running, in under 15 minutes, as compared to 45 minutes or more using the old method of pulling liquid paper stock off the machine. As other crews watched and learned, they came up with their own innovations for attaining similar "on the fly" product changes.

At any point, the mentor could have disturbed the process by overdissecting the idea, offering too much guidance, or trying to standardize the procedure once a particular crew came up with the "best" way of accomplishing the task. Also, I would suggest that the mentor could have stifled the process by offering *no* guidance, which could have led to unsafe or destructive practices on the machine. Offering no guidance also might have suggested a lack of interest.

Instead, my boss offered latitude and created innovation, all by simply setting a few straightforward parameters. In the end, his time parameter of 30 minutes became the time to beat, rather than a goal to meet. Freedom in structure.

Here's another example. Once every two weeks, on that same paper machine, our plant would shut down for *conditioning*—essentially a good cleaning and repairing. During these half-day conditionings, we would dictate and schedule what each worker had to do down to the minute. As Murphy (you know, the guy who wrote that Law) would have it, unforeseen problems would arise, people would have to be pulled off other tasks, and the highly intensive work table would fall apart. Eventually, our team came up with a very loose schedule of tasks. As long as the tasks were accomplished, the crews could pair up any way they liked and complete the jobs in any manner or order. Again, the positive results were staggering. Machine conditionings were accomplished in about two-thirds of the time scheduled on the original, complicated time lines. More potential machine problems were unearthed and addressed. People teamed up with those they got along with and got more done. Again, by formulating time and task standards—but stopping there—managers were setting goals to be met and times to be beaten. The result was a parade of energy and innovation. Freedom in structure.

One final example. A large company I worked for once purchased and took over a small concern in Scotland. A few years after the merger, I met with a few of the Scottish executive officers, visiting the States for management training.

"So how does it feel to be a part of our company?" I asked one of the more junior managers.

"Actually," he responded, "I don't feel much of anything."

"How so?"

"Well," he continued, "when our company was first purchased, we expected a hoard of Americans to invade our facility, telling us what to do and how to do it. Up to this point, aside from an occasional visit from our division director, we've been pretty much left alone. He hands us our yearly goals, some guidelines that he deems important, and we do our best, by ourselves, to meet them." Ahhhh, freedom in structure.

Keep in mind that the emphasis here is on the setting of clearly understood parameters—not on the autonomy it generates. I'm not convinced that giving your apprentices a chaotic work environment produces anything more than more chaos. Oh, people might look busy. There might be the light of kinetic energy and dust in the air. But it's more the illusory lighting and smoke of a magic show rather than anything getting accomplished. Without an explicit set of objectives and constraints in place to harness the independence of your disciples, even the most energetic and spirited pupil will flounder.

As John Pastor suggests, "Let people know the rules—so that they can beat them!"

How unfortunate that today's business world embraces the blurry lines of poorly defined control and boundaries. Many people I know, particularly in large organizations, hold distaste for authoritative rule and suggest that potent leaders are distant leaders. Yes, the strong mentor may, at times, come off as aloof, especially if he subscribes to the synergy of separateness. But is the distant leader the unapproachable leader?

My argument is that the forceful but somewhat removed mentor is the most approachable person you will ever meet, especially if he is still in a decision-making mode.

Look at the opposite end of the spectrum. Think for a moment about your company's geeky project managers. Here are would-be team leaders, often brand new, given projects to research and plan but usually not the power to implement. When they come trolling around your work area, asking annoying questions, taking copious notes, do *you* want to speak to them? Probably not. Why? Because they usually don't have the power to carry out their plans. Sure, they may have the ear of the person who does—but why not cut out the middleman?

My point is—with all due respect to geeky project managers—that, if used properly, well-defined mentor power can promote openness. Your disciples will appreciate when their feedback is listened to and taken into consideration by someone truly in charge that seems to have their best interests at heart. And the freedom you offer through the structure you provide will create for those disciples a surrounding of individual responsibility and growth.

DON'T BE AFRAID TO SET GOOD PEOPLE FREE

I remember a mentor of mine once saying to me, "Scott, don't get too caught up in the art of job preservation. Remember, if they can't fire you, then they also can't promote you." Wise words from a wise man. His observation was interesting in two respects.

First, there *was* a lot of self-preservation going on in my company. Some managers and administrators were taking great pains to retailor their jobs in such ways as to make themselves appear indispensable. The fact that this senior person recognized these goings-ons not only showed his insight but perhaps also hinted at the futility of their efforts.

Second, his comment was interesting in that, by mentioning promotion, he was admitting a potentially uncomfortable aspect of mentoring: the people who get the most out of mentoring—and who therefore are most likely to enrich the team—are often the first to leave the team and the mentor through promotion or otherwise. A gifted person that you take time to instruct and inspire is simply not going to be around the team or the organization for long.

So what are you, the mentor, to do? Should you give up creating your own defensive strategies aimed at keeping good people around? Should you bother to develop and mentor gifted people if you only are going to lose them in the process?

The answer is *yes!*, you should enthusiastically mentor the good people in your organization and, yes, you should enthusiastically set them free when other opportunities present themselves—even opportunities outside your team or even at another company.

Why does the mentoring process need to include, or at least accept, the notion of setting good people free? There are three practical reasons you need to acknowledge, and perhaps even openly discuss, the possibility of promotion or career moves with your disciples.

Acknowledging the next good thing

Your disciple will be a lot more relaxed and willing to learn from you if you simply acknowledge that something better will someday come along. If you both openly discuss the possibility that new opportunities are on the horizon, you put to rest any discomfort over hidden agendas or lack of loyalty. After all, most good people do not aspire to be the best machine operator or the best administrator or the best lower tier manager forever. A wonderful employee is always in training for the *next* good thing to come along. Put the disciple at ease that she doesn't have to feel guilty or embarrassed about reaching for the brass ring. There is nothing wrong with people developing themselves for future positions.

Surely there are folks in your organization going to school at nights or pursuing college education in some other nontraditional manner. Are these people working a full-time job while maintaining a college schedule simply because they want to be better at what they are *currently* doing? Perhaps. There's nothing wrong with simple self-improvement, and expansion of knowledge for its own sake is certainly a noble prospect. On the other hand, as someone who has worked a full-time job while carrying a full graduate course load, I can assure you that there are probably grander notions in the minds of these people. Working while going to school is not easy, and those willing to endure its rigors usually have their designs on a bigger lot in life. Whether it's a high-school equivalency certificate or a college degree or some type of certification or licensing—people seek these things because of the promise they bring.

If the organization is lucky, perhaps one or two of these self-enriching people will seek management positions. As mentioned earlier, as job descriptions and empowerment become more and more muddled, if anyone is seeking to be a boss, she's a gift to the team.

Fortunately for me, I have had bosses and mentors who brought up the topic of advancement out of the team early on in the relationship. One of my first jobs out of high school was writing news copy at a small radio station. I remember my boss telling me he expected me to learn everything I could about the job—and then move on to a bigger station making more money! Surprisingly, he stated this fact with pride. "I've trained some of the best names in the news business," he boasted. Never mind that none of these people still worked at his station. The fact that he was developing good news writers and setting them free gave *him* a sense of esteem and fulfillment.

At another company, the human resources director often would say, "Hey, we know the deal—you learn here and you move on." His candor was refreshing, and it made his career-advancing advice all the more discerning.

The bottom line is that by freely admitting to and bringing up the potential for advancement, you display your relaxed nature and sincerity as a mentor.

Looking past the horizon

The second reason for mentoring in spite of losing good people is that our students, if they are to be properly developed, need to see past their current horizons. In other words, if the people you mentor are not already focused on their potential, then *you as mentor* should focus them on it. You should plant in your people's minds the notions of promotions and advancement. You should put the thoughts in their minds that, down the road, they can do bigger and better things with their lives. Why? Because people always try harder when their sights are set higher.

Keeping your disciples focused on the future is a wonderful way to keep them grounded in the present. Is a college basketball coach concerned about whether or not one or two of his ball players make the pros? Yes. Advancement of his finest players into the NBA is a good thing for the players and for the reputation of the college's sports program. But is that coach's primary mission developing those players for the NBA? Certainly not. He is worried about putting together a winning college basketball team. However, by mentoring his star people towards the ultimate goal of attaining pro contracts, he controls their outlook and, therefore, their actions in the present.

Sometimes good people stay

The third reason for mentoring good people despite the prospect of losing them is that openly discussing with them the possibility of leaving the team does not necessary *mean* they will. Sometimes people find the self-development and personal fulfillment they desire right where they are. Feelings of esteem, recognition, and prestige do not have to be limited to places outside the team. Promotion within the team, pay adjustments for accomplishment, and acknowledgment of good performance go a long way towards retaining good people. Although, as a mentor, you may not be directly responsible for promotions or raises, you should make sure that the people who give out the promotions and raises are aware of a good disciple's performance.

As for acknowledgment of a job well done, you can probably handle much of this responsibility yourself. Remember that true recognition of success is a shared experience, as hard workers are appreciated for their accomplishments in front of their peers. For me, any honor I have received—whether it was getting an Army medal pinned on, or receiving a degree, or being handed an achievement award or getting a promotion—has meant something strongly positive mostly because it was happening in front of my peers.

Isn't it possible that some people stay on your team—in ironic fashion—just because you recognize the possibility of losing them? By conceding this plausibility, you essentially are telling your disciples "Hey, you are good enough to be sought by others." Such an admission is the ultimate compliment to a hard worker, and many times, just knowing that others appreciate her level of performance is enough to keep her around.

Bringing up the possibility of people leaving can be very disarming. I remember a colleague—having a tough time with an unruly team—once saying, "I know many of you are upset with me and have sent resumes out to a headhunter. He told me so while I was submitting my own resume!" The statement was humorous enough—from what I was told—to take the edge off a tense work environment, and since he was the one who broached the idea of leaving the company, he dampened the notion as a secret way of expressing exasperation. As it turned out, no one on his team left, and they muscled through their growing pains together. By recognizing the team's dissension and openly touching on the possibility of people leaving, I believe he removed the mystique of fleeing and made people think more rationally.

One final thought on setting good people free. By openly discussing the potential for advancement out of the team, you promote an honest comparison between what else exists for your disciples and what they currently have. Often, people grow to appreciate and become more enthusiastic about their current positions after screening other opportunities and offers outside the organization. I actually have helped people on my team prepare for promotion interviews within the company, knowing that it might mean losing them. But I felt that if a team member considered me approachable enough as a mentor to discuss the possibility of leaving the team, I should offer him interviewing techniques in the same way I had offered technical advice or work advice.

So don't be protective of your people or selfish with your mentoring advice. By not being afraid to set good people free, you create a set of disciples that—while they're around—will make you and your team sparkle.

KNOW WHAT'S IN IT FOR YOU

Ron Green knows more about mentoring than most of us do. On three different occasions in his career, he has been asked by the U.S. Army to command a Special Operations company of soldiers. "I think I've reached the flat part of the learning curve," he quips. Green's colleagues cite a tireless man who spends a comparatively disproportionate amount of his time counseling and training his lieutenants one-on-one.

So what's in it for the mentor who takes lots of his precious time to develop a few exceptional team members? First, says Green, there's the personal sense of accomplishment that comes from seeing people advance. "I have no problem living vicariously through the successes of my subordinates," he says. "As far as personal fulfillment goes, I view each one of their achievements—in a sense—as if it were my own."

The second, not-so-internal benefit to mentoring is that people tend to see Green through the accomplishments of his team. "Undeniably, it's self-promotion," he claims proudly. "You definitely promote yourself by promoting others toward success."

What else is in it for you, the mentor, aside from living both vicariously and openly through the successes of your disciples? Are there selfish advantages to be gained by taking the time to guide others? Sure.

Developing others means developing yourself

By mentoring, you can't help but improve yourself as a manager. Nothing makes a person more tuned in to self-improvement than recommending means of improving to others. Good advice requires forethought and preparation—sometimes lots of it. Such advice might involve research, analysis, and personal reflection. After all, a good mentor doesn't just blather silly advice but instead offers sound counsel as a master of the topic at hand. If you are to approach a disciple's questions on, say, career development, you already should have considered these questions on a personal level—assessing your own career development and the steps you followed and continue to follow along the way toward your own advancements. What things worked? What career decisions caused setbacks? What decisions ultimately brought career fulfillment and happiness to your life? Are you there yet? What's going on in the world that can get you there? Accepting the idea that disciples will be coming to you for advice, you become obligated to take the time and effort to develop—and master—decision paths for yourself.

I once had a team member who openly desired promotion into a management job in another manufacturing department. Believing in the concept of setting good people free, I suggested to him some ways he could position himself more assertively towards getting that promotion. One recommendation was to create a resume-like list of recent accomplishments and then provide that list to the department supervisor he hoped to work for someday, possibly even updating the list periodically. My lesson to him: selling oneself, even within one's own organization, can be almost as important as doing a consistently good job. As it turned out, not long after I had offered him that advice, I decided to follow it myself. I created a monthly newsletter to my team, letting them know how well they had performed the previous month and what new, innovative things they had achieved. Choosing a few people within the company I was hoping to work for someday, I ensured that each of them received a copy of my newsletter. This bulletin served many positive purposes. It helped *sell* the team on themselves, as they took account, in writing, of the good things they had done recently. It allowed me a written chronicle of my team's success. And, again, it opened up a subtle way to let others know of my achievements as a manager—and as something of team cheerleader. Most importantly, it was a small, self-promoting gesture that evolved from giving advice to another person.

Good mentoring ultimately translates into mentoring yourself.

Mentoring helps you choose
your successor

Hey, you're not going to be around forever—or at least not in your current position. Why not use the process of mentoring to help select the person who might replace you? Let mentoring be a part of your legacy.

Ramsay-Gerding company vice-president Tom Gerding says mentoring is often doing for another what has already been done for you. "My mentor has been the founder of our company, Dale Ramsay," he says. "He took me into the field and taught me construction management from a hands-on perspective I hadn't yet seen. Now it's *my* turn to carry on that training." Gerding makes no bones about looking for the person who might someday take his place. "There's no success without a successor," he says.

Unrestricted mentoring induces loyalty

Ron Green offers the most fortunate side effect to mentoring people up to their next assignments: loyalty from your disciples. "Advising people to the point that you're advancing them out the door creates an atmosphere of indebted loyalty," he says. "You can ask people to work long hours and to make all kinds of sacrifices. If they sense deep down that you care for them personally, they will always be devoted to you and your objectives."

Green adds that most people hold a very sensitive radar when it comes to detecting caring bosses. In other words, if you say you're interested in helping disciples advance their careers, you'd better mean it because they'll know if you're bluffing.

Mentoring means control

Another benefit to mentoring is its control aspect. As you influence the attitude of your disciples, you hold the practical advantage of affecting (and effecting) the actions of others. If your ultimate goal is to direct the activities of your team towards organizational objectives, then certainly mentoring can be appreciated for its internal influence. As you guide others in their personal development, you guide them in their conduct and perspectives. In the process of becoming good disciples, your followers also become good workers—useful, integral parts of the team. It may be somewhat self-serving, but it certainly is not selfish for a manager to advance the team while advancing the individual needs of its members. Again, by controlling the outlook of your disciples, you control their actions.

Controlling people's outlook and actions—isn't that what managing is all about? And, unfortunately, isn't that what many managers hope to accomplish when they call another useless meeting to order? Mentoring is a wonderful tool that compels you to address the human side of managing. It propels you into beneficial, one-on-one encounters and, as a result, forces you away from staff meetings.

SUMMARY

- Mentoring should be rediscovered as managers take people under their wings and provide guidance and early career development. Managers should embrace the concept from the disciple's view as they look for their own mentors, and from the mentor's view as they select their own disciples.

- Mentoring is better than any group meeting in controlling people's outlooks and actions.

- The ideal mentor is open, eager to listen, generally accessible, and well prepared with topical advice.

- When selecting their disciples, mentors should consider who is the most interested in their guidance, who stands to gain the most, and who can best help the team.

- By providing structure and parameters, mentors paradoxically offer their disciples freedom. Once freed from having to find their limits, people will exercise creativity and innovation in order to stay within a provided set of guidelines.

- By training disciples for advancement away from the team, the mentor develops the best people *in* a team.

- Mentoring others ultimately translates into mentoring oneself.

CHAPTER 9

Avoid the Meetings of Others

KNOW HOW TO HANDLE OTHER PEOPLE'S MEETINGS

Okay, so you've seen the light and you've given up holding meetings. You now understand why meetings don't work. And you've decided to emphasize one-on-one management, organizational channeling, delegating, and a strong, hands-on leadership style to purge yourself of the unnecessary daily get-togethers that have controlled your life.

So why are you still going to meetings?

Ah, yes—you're not the only one in your organization who convenes meetings. In fact, you're invited to lots of other people's meetings, and sometimes the request for your presence is an offer you can't refuse.

Up to this point, the emphasis of this book has been on how to avoid calling your own meetings—and for good reason. As with any fundamental change, the inclination of an organization away from standard workplace meetings is most likely to happen when important people within the organization want it to be so. In other words, my hope in writing this book is to change not only *your* attitude towards meetings, but also the attitudes of the people most likely to *invite* you.

That being said, there is no reason why someone—like yourself—who is unlikely to call meetings should acquiesce to every meeting invitation he is given. Furthermore, there are ways to ensure that the number of meetings (mandatory and voluntary) you are asked to attend is reduced.

How can you avoid the meetings called by others without appearing indifferent or negligent? And how can you change other people's inclinations to call groups together? Let's talk about how to properly avoid attending the meetings held by others.

Stay busy and productive

Staying busy will make you less likely to get selected for a useless meeting. Now, I'm not suggesting that you simply pretend to look busy in order to avoid getting "volunteered." But I *am* suggesting that people who attempt to fill their day with productive, meaningful activity are less likely to get designated to address purposeless topics at tedious meetings.

Many companies are obligated by their operating headquarters to hold meetings on a myriad of topics. Often, the moderator must report back to HQ on what was covered and what (supposedly) was accomplished. There are many misconceptions and wrong reasons for mandating these meetings. Every company has its fill of MBA-types—some who never have seen an organization at its working levels—trying to influence the organization via long-distance policy making. Some of them feel very strongly that these policies actually will make a positive difference. Others may have less shallow reasoning, such as trying to make their mark in a visible way (a bullet for their annual evaluation forms). In either case, if they cannot be with the people they are hoping to influence, they can at least force them together for meetings, provide the moderators with instructions, and request documentation on what happened.

The obligations sent down from corporate headquarters rarely serve the successful, hands-on manager as little more than nuisances. If an organization is told to bring 10 people together to discuss some nonsensical topic, what is the smart manager going to do? That's right—he's going to find the 10 people who yield the *least* amount of impact from getting pulled away from their jobs. The key is to *not* be one of those 10 people chosen. By staying energetic and fruitful, you avoid being selected for such meetings.

As a salesman earlier in my career, I worked in three different sales offices where the leading rep was regularly excused from the useless meetings the rest of us were called to attend. In each case, it was understood that since she was off closing big deals and bringing money into the company, she did not have to bother herself with sitting in on a purposeless meeting (and they were *all* purposeless). What was the unspoken message at these sales offices? *If you produce the numbers that she produces, we won't waste your time at these meetings either.* It was a message I took to heart, as I aspired to bring my sales figures to a level that would unofficially exempt me from attending the tiresome ramblings of a sales manager.

As a production manager and operations manager later in my career, there were still those hands-on, indispensable people who—everyone understood—could not be bothered with meetings. I am thinking specifically of two people. One was an assistant production supervisor who was usually off somewhere "putting out fires." His presence at meetings was rarely required. Another person was a mechanical engineer who was responsible for starting up new, automated machine systems. Again, the importance of his tending to these systems prevailed over his filling a seat at a daily, valueless meeting. No one ever questioned his absence.

Remember, every organization has that *can do* person who is neither invited to nor expected to attend meetings, simply because it is understood that she is off somewhere tending to something important. The key is to make yourself one of those needed players—one of those people whose mission, productivity, and results transcend the obligation to attend the useless meetings of others.

Clarify your job description and duties

Conveying that you are too busy to attend meetings does not have to be achieved entirely through major accomplishments or through other, blatant displays of bustling activity. Simply connecting yourself to a clear job description goes a long way in clarifying your unavailability at meetings. It has been said that any good job-offer letter should include a list of responsibilities. So what is wrong with periodically spelling out your job duties? Get with your supervisor and explain that you would like to review your everyday obligations.

My operations experience includes managing a shipping warehouse, where I made it clear to everyone that from 7:30 A.M. to 1:00 P.M., I was unavailable for all meetings and all training. I usually was not rude or headstrong about this unavailability (although such displays did happen from time to time). However, I was resolute in staying at my primary workstation during those hours. The reason was that we had several large, important customers who needed their orders on time and, without my presence at the shipping docks, the likelihood of orders not getting shipped out as they should was greatly increased. That is not to say other people were unable to handle these tasks or that delegating was not taking place. But there were inevitable quality issues and logistical issues that, as a manager, I needed to be around to address. There were certain "fires" that I could put out the fastest. My availability to the shipping area from 7:30 A.M. to 1:00 P.M. ensured that trucks during those hours and throughout the rest of the day would leave on time.

As the person in charge of this operation, I wrote down all those things that I was responsible for making happen during a typical shipping day, including those logistical problems I normally had to resolve. I organized these obligations on a word processor, and I presented them briefly to my boss. By encountering her and clarifying my job description and duties, I not only enlightened her as to the many things I made happen, but I also got her support for missing (or, better still, not being invited to) morning meetings.

Again, sometimes all it takes to get yourself excused from useless conferences is to spell out the requirements and obligations of your job.

Respectfully excuse yourself

I have watched people perform all sorts of rituals in their attempts to get out of meetings. I saw a manager avoid answering his telephone on meeting days, figuring that if no one could get in touch with him he couldn't get called to meetings. A coworker of mine used to ensure that the meeting she was conducting carried over into the scheduled time for another meeting she was expected to attend somewhere else. She figured that the ultimate excuse for missing a meeting was her presence at another one. So what is an uncomplicated alternative to this scheming? How about respectfully excusing yourself? "I'm sorry, but I have other things today that are more pressing. I will not be at that meeting."

Excusing yourself might be met with all kinds of resistance—but then again, it might not. One less person at a senseless meeting will not make it any less senseless. And if enough people excuse themselves from a scheduled meeting covering a fruitless topic, then perhaps the person calling the meeting will get the message and will use the time previously set aside to tend to something more useful.

My mother is a senior nurse at a hospital—I can't figure out how she still has the energy! Her title is "shift charge nurse," meaning that she not only has patients in a hospital wing to deal with, but she also has to supervise nurses in that wing as well. Mom has excused herself from staff meetings for years, particularly meetings where new policies are covered or current policies are clarified. Her response when invited: "I will not be attending, but I will review the minutes in detail." And since the minutes of most meetings are e-mailed en masse to all supervisors, she has access to those notes almost immediately. "Rarely do I read anything that makes me wish I had attended," she observes.

Unlike myself, Mom has no heartfelt leadership philosophies against meetings. She just finds them a bad investment of her time, and she is too damned busy to show up. Very rarely do others challenge her for excusing herself.

Make sure that when you attempt to excuse yourself, you do so respectfully. Remember that the key is to free up your time—not to butt heads with other people or to come off as negligent or belligerent. If there's no way to excuse oneself in a respectful manner, then don't do it.

The idea of excluding yourself from a meeting might seem uncomfortable. But consider another uncomfortable idea. How many people in your organization over the years have missed promotions or—in the long run—have been fired for bad performance because they allowed meetings to overcome them, clogging their workday and impeding their achievements? Have you become, or are you becoming, one of those people?

Make yourself accessible

Bosses often call needless meetings as personnel roundups, somehow associating head counts with influence and supervision. In a way, I do not blame them. When task assignments and management obligations become overwhelming, managers easily can imagine a correlation between personnel accessibility and command influence. By making yourself available to others—using such modes of communication as wireless telephones, pagers, voice mail, e-mail, etc.—you do your part in keeping meeting time down to a minimum.

Set the example

With all things in life, actions speak considerably louder than words. Setting the example for others in everything you do can have the most impact on how others behave around you and towards you. As you manage your team without meetings, do not be surprised if you gain considerable attention and emulation. The impression you leave starts with the example you set—employing one-on-one management, strong leadership, organizational channeling, delegating—each and every day.

Compare meeting reduction to weight reduction. After several grand—but empty—announcements, I once decided to get serious about losing some weight. My brother Andrew and I chose a particular regimen of food and exercise. We decided to push each other with a set goal (amount of weight lost by a certain date) and a gentlemen's wager. And I set about the business of losing weight.

After about 20 pounds lost, people at work began to notice. Several of them casually asked what program I was on. As I passed 30 pounds lost, there was some praise at work and at home—again, no great hubbub.

So where did the real complimenting originate? It came from the actions of others. My boss—who had asked impassively about my diet and exercising—went on a similar program and lost a noticeable amount of weight. On several occasions, he came to me and enthusiastically discussed his success. At least two other people at work followed suit. Assuming that imitation is a high form of flattery, I felt truly flattered.

Think for a moment. Suppose that I had suggested to my boss, in the nicest possible way, that he needed to lose some weight, perhaps handing him a diet and exercise plan to follow. Is it likely that he would have undertaken the project—or, if he had, is it likely that I still would have been in his good graces?

As with weight loss or anything else, the example you set managing without meetings will serve as the ultimate influence on other people—and will have the greatest reciprocal effect when you start getting invited to fewer meetings.

Obtain the meeting itinerary early and offer answers beforehand

If a meeting has been called, see if you can find out as quickly as possible what the meeting will cover. If an itinerary has been written, try to obtain a copy. There is a good chance that, if you can provide the meeting chairperson with the information he's requesting in advance, you will be excused from attending. One of the reasons people gather others into the conference room is to feel that they have influence—or perhaps just to make sure somebody cares what they have to say. By inquiring what is on a person's mind and reacting promptly to his request for information and input, you put his mind at ease regarding his prestige. And you show you care. Sometimes that is all a meeting marshal needs.

Directly approach someone with your antimeeting philosophy

Be respectful, not confrontational. But, hey, state your case. People often do what they do merely because no one has extended an alternative to them. Remember that law of physics regarding objects in motion staying in motion unless they meet resistance? People are no different. Oftentimes they hold meetings because no one has ever suggested another way. Perhaps encountering people with your candid thoughts might be an appropriate tactic to nudge them off their steadfast course of meetings, meetings, meetings. Offer them some alternatives. Tell them what *you* do. Sell people on your antimeeting philosophy.

Use positive reinforcement. Compliment the person who avoids holding unnecessary meetings. I always make a point of thanking someone for completing a project or soliciting information without holding the obligatory meeting.

Voice your displeasure following an unproductive meeting

Yes, they are *all* unproductive. Nevertheless, at the end of a particularly long, meandering, painfully boring and excruciatingly inconclusive meeting, why not articulate your disappointment over how the meeting was conducted? Don't put on a show. Just find the person who ran the meeting and privately voice your professional opinion. "Perhaps next time," you might suggest, "we could set some meeting goals and some time limits, and maybe we could force ourselves to stick to the agenda a little better than we did today." Admittedly, if someone senior to yourself—especially your boss—has had a large role in this badly run meeting, you might be sticking your rear end a little too far into the breeze. But if the meeting was largely made up of your contemporaries, by all means speak up. After all, it is *your* time and productivity getting wasted.

Besides, even if speaking up does not have the positive long-term effect of reducing the number of long meetings held, it might have the short-term effect of keeping meetings shorter and more focused—and that is certainly not a failure. If the average person at a meeting earns $42,000 a year, then each hour that person spends at the meeting costs the company a little over 20 dollars an hour. Therefore, 10 people at a two-hour-long meeting cost the company more than 400 dollars (plus lost production). Did the last meeting you attend net the company 400 dollars worth of results?

Offer the person a substitute agenda. If there are other ways to accomplish the stated objective of a meeting, why not offer up these alternatives as meeting substitutes? In the mid-1990s, the State of New York provided grant money to some companies to have quality control trainers come in and instruct the lower-to-middle management staff. And so, a state-funded quality control guru came to us with his worksheets and charts—and enough meetings (attendance was mandatory) to break the spirit of even the most enthusiastic team player.

Once, I observed aloud that this gentleman only had visited the administrative side of our mill; he had never made it as far as the blenders and the refiners and the machines and the dryers. "Wouldn't it be useful," I offered, "if we took you on a tour of the mill and listened to your suggestions along the way?"

His spurious response: "I purposely have avoided visiting your workplace. I would rather offer you the theory behind quality control and have you apply it to your particular areas yourselves." Oh brother!

After some further coaxing, he acquiesced to tour the mill with us and to make some on-site observations and recommendations. Sure, our initial intent in suggesting the tour was to get the hell out of the conference room. But after putting forth this alternative agenda and showing him the areas where we conducted our daily management, he did, in fact, make a few noteworthy suggestions. As a result, another meeting was avoided, and something happened that instead proved to be productive and worthwhile.

Therefore, the alternative agenda served two purposes: 1) getting a meeting-weary group of people out of the conference room, and 2) discovering problems and considering hands-on recommendations that never could have been ascertained in the sterile surroundings of a forced-attendance meeting.

Refuse offering vehicles of comfort

Ah, what cozy gastronomical events some workplace meetings are. Doughnuts and coffee or, if later in the day, pizza and soda are sometimes provided.

These small, hedonistic comforts undoubtedly are meant to both attract people to the meeting and to somehow reward those people who acquiesce to its unpleasantness.

I say that if you have anything to do with what will be provided at a meeting, think twice before offering the types of goodies that might get people cozy and eager to stay, ramble on, and accomplish nothing.

Furthermore, I suggest convening the meeting in an atmosphere of, well, discomfort. Conference areas are often air-conditioned meccas, located far from people's normal work areas where they cannot be seen or bothered. It is no wonder that so much dead wood gravitates towards such surroundings.

I say *Don't build it, and they won't come!* In other words, if you have anything to do with where a meeting is to be held, make the meeting place practical, not relaxing,

If you happen to work in a manufacturing environment, there is a chance that the layout of your factory includes both a production center and an administrative center. If you are a manufacturer being urged (or forced) by an administrator to conduct meetings on a particular topic, I suggest that you convene your meetings in the production center rather than in the comfortable conference rooms of the administrative building. No one will fault you for wanting to meet near the place where you and other production managers do business. It will keep things less cozy and isolated. But more importantly, it will probably keep the administrator who is insisting on such meetings from attending. I have known many production people and many administrative people, and they are rarely at ease in each other's surroundings (even though many of them have worked in both venues). By keeping away the person that asked for the meeting in first place, you are able to make the conference short or cancel it altogether and attend to more important things.

Assume the role of project manager

Many meetings stem from the assigned projects or pet projects of others. If you see a project on the horizon, and you see the potential for many, many useless meetings as its result, there may be several advantages to taking over the project yourself. If for no other reason, taking on the project allows you to decide what meetings, if any, are appropriate.

Let's expand on this tenth way of avoiding the meetings of others.

TAKE OVER THE PROJECT

Taking on a project and assuming a leadership role in completing it means that *you* are in control. Therefore, you can decide how required work is delegated and how information is disseminated. In other words, you govern the productive time and you stand in the way of unproductive time—and if you want to run the project without ever holding a useless meeting, chances are that you will be allowed to do so.

I am not suggesting you look for projects that might not otherwise have been undertaken; there is no sense in creating work for yourself unless it is something you feel passionate about and something you believe will help the organization. What I *am* proposing is that you take on a project that *needs* to get finished, one that probably will involve your time and effort anyway. If you are going to get sucked into the vortex of an important team undertaking, you might as well manage the time and resources required for completing it. Along with this positive, personal control, there is also the benefit of experience you'll get managing a project, such as endeavoring into facets of the organization outside the realm of your current job description. Also, managing a project successfully will get you noticed in an organization—in a good way. And finally, such an undertaking, when proudly followed from beginning to end, allows you to enjoy a sense of accomplishment generally not associated with the more mundane aspects of your job. As psychologists often point out, it is the sense of attainment that brings about job satisfaction—even more so than money, believe it or not.

So how do you assume the role of project manager? The first step is to determine the impact of a likely project on your organization. What is the return on the investment of your time and resources? Does the project affect the bottom line? Does it improve efficiency? Are there other, less quantifiable benefits? Does the project improve worker morale? Does it improve customer service? Are the benefits immediate or will they be seen in the long run?

Do people take on projects without first gauging their impact? Yes, constantly. For example, I have seen several manufacturing environments where the daily mantra is "Speed up the machines!" It is often a shortsighted slogan because anyone who has worked on an assembly line or in a continuous production setting knows that simply speeding up machines—without giving the entire process extensive consideration—is a recipe for disaster. And yet there is always that new project engineer, wanting to be the hero, who sees fit to turn a knob or two without checking with anyone first. The process goes to hell and, lo and behold, the MEETINGS begin—usually with the engineer at the head of the table, trying to figure out what on earth went wrong. If this gifted young person would have followed some practical tenets for gathering information from individual, experienced operators, the problems associated with these machine speed-up projects might have been anticipated. In other words, the engineer was not fully considering the impact of the endeavor.

By volunteering your time as a project manager in this example, you would become situated at the helm, where the impact of your team's current and future efforts could be anticipated. Does the benefit of running the machines more quickly—which presumably creates more product and therefore makes the big bosses happier—outweigh the costs, such as a less-smooth-running operation, more wear and tear on the machinery, or more defective product? Assuming people will be put to task to speed up these systems, can they be "sold" on the project? Is there a demand for the additional product generated? If not, does the fixed cost of machine downtime justify the faster speeds they're running at? Do the energy resources required to speed up the machinery (power, steam, etc.) cost more or less than the benefit gained from the additional speed?

By serving as project leader and gauging the impact of a project, you may be in a position to call it off when it becomes apparent that the costs outweigh the benefits—and before any wet-behind-the-ears engineer can begin screwing things up and wasting everyone's time holding useless meetings.

If the potential impact of a project appears encouraging, your next step as project manager is to determine its scope. How far does this project reach? Does it carry into different departments—perhaps different locations? What is its timetable? Does it have a conclusion? What are its long-term and short-term goals? Is this scope manageable?

I remember my company's director of operations once choosing to take control of the plant where I worked rather than promoting anyone into the plant manager job or taking a chance on someone coming in "cold" from another company. He took the unusual step of declaring himself the new plant manager and tackling these problems himself. On the surface, the move seemed like folly. How could someone embark upon the task of creating such a large visit as a "visiting" plant manager? But, looking back, his actions were a stroke of time-management genius. First, he addressed some the plant's problems as a consolidated picture, rather than a series of random and isolated difficulties. He saw the potential resolution of these problems as an assignment with results that he—either directly or indirectly—would be accountable for demonstrating to the company. He appraised the project for magnitude, time, and manageability. He set goals and deadlines, and he established an agenda for visiting the plant to check up on everyone's progress. Clearly, in his judgment, the significance of this project warranted his personal attention, but the scope of the project was still within the reins of his hands-on management style. I believe his efforts were very effective. Each day that he visited the plant, he walked from one end of the facility to the other, asking questions of individuals and writing down personal observations. He was the very proactive, matter-of-fact manager that was called for at the time. And when the project was complete and he felt it was time to turn over the reigns to a recruited manager, he was able to conduct the transition from a standpoint of hands-on knowledge.

By volunteering your time as a project manager, you put yourself in a position not only to answer questions about the project's scope but also to modify its scope to make it more attainable or practical. You may determine that its reach makes it unrealistic for your organization to embrace. However, if a project seems realistic enough, and if you decide to volunteer your time and take it on, then you might be empowered by *your* management to determine its timeline and deadline. You might be permitted to set goals and establish measurements of success. You might be allowed to select those individuals who will help you in bringing this effort to a successful conclusion.

From there, you use the process of organizational channeling to carry out the mission while reducing the need for meetings (and therefore reducing the demand for your presence at meetings).

One more thought on using project management as a meeting buffer. When I was working on my master's degree, I was often given homework *for* work. That is, knowing I was an employed manager, several professors assigned me the task of finding things at work where the potential for improvement existed. I was asked to research a particular problem at my place of business, create a hypothetical solution, apply the solution, and then measure the results using standard prescripts under the Scientific Method. In a sense, I was asked to manage a project. At first, I approached these assignments just as a means of completing homework and getting a grade. But then something significant happened. I found myself taking an interest in these projects outside the realm of simply generating a college report. In the end, some of the solutions I found to problems are still being used. I looked at ways to improve the packaging of our company's product before being shipped overseas. I looked at new ways to delegate work and budget time in my department. I studied absenteeism, catalogued it, and considered ways to reduce it. In sum, I found myself fascinated with projects that had started out only as homework. Why? My guess is that I became captivated because these activities were taking me outside the mundane aspects of my job, to include work scheduling, "putting out fires," and, of course, attending meetings.

As mentioned earlier, the project manager serves many various roles. By willingly taking on these roles, you place yourself in charge of much of your time and energy, and you convey the message to others that you are getting something constructive done and, no thank you, you do not have time for their useless meetings.

LET RAW INTERACTION TAKE OVER

People often convene meetings due to a perceived absence of communication, along with the poor assumption that meetings will open up the lines of interaction. It may be difficult to change the latter misconception, but it certainly is possible to adjust the former. That is, if you convince people around you that the lines of communication are wide open and effective, you will go a long way toward keeping the spores of executive apprehension from mushrooming into needless meetings at the workplace.

It *is* possible for meetings to become extinct in an organization that finds a comfort level without them. There are those rare managers who proclaim, "Hey, meetings aren't a problem in my company. We just don't need them, and we just don't have them." And what is the number-one reason they give for not needing meetings? "We get the word out just fine without them."

I have already addressed the benefits of effective, alternative means of communication, and I have put forward the argument that meetings hinder, not help, the communication situation. Now let's talk about perceptions. Convincing people about the pointlessness of their meetings entails not only the existence of time wasted but also the *acknowledgement* of its existence. Conversely, you not only have to practice good communication to make people feel at ease about scrapping meetings, but you have to *convince others* that information and feedback are getting swiftly disseminated.

So what conveys this image of a thriving exchange of ideas, and how can you help bring about this appearance? When I think of good, consistent communication within an organization, three symptoms come to mind: high energy, high enthusiasm, and high volume. These symptoms are instantly recognizable and, fortunately, they are all contagious. As you keep your team members and your bosses abreast of what is going on in your department, approach them with vigor. Stay effervescent! Be loud—almost obnoxiously so. In these times of multimedia sensory overload, someone who cranks up the volume when he walks into a room is sure to create or heighten an aura of connecting thoughts and ideas. And while you're at it, enjoy being the center of attention, especially when it is good news that you are broadcasting. Meetings are often called when people perceive shared information as stagnant. So get rid of these worries over stagnation. Stir things up! Your motivation is sure to catch on.

People also tend to convene meetings because they believe it is the only way to gather current, useful information. Paranoia over the availability of information will bring a nervous manager to the meeting table at the drop of a dime. The solution is opening up your work routine, your daily goals, your successes and any gained knowledge to all those who might benefit from the information, as well as making sure they *know* this data is on hand. In spite of the commonly held belief that holding back information fosters job preservation, the reality is that managers appreciate people whose daily progress at work is an open book, and they detest people who are miserly with work-related facts, figures, and findings. Making your routine—and the results it produces—readily available will put your boss at ease and reduce her perceived need for meetings.

Make sure this data is organized, perhaps even catalogued if enough of it exists. If your company has a "shared files" computer network, add any useful and appropriate information as a shared file. Your openness often will be appreciated, and you likely will help others do their job with the news and info you provide.

Along with making information accessible, try to make *yourself* accessible as well. Bosses often call needless meetings as personnel roundups, associating head counts with influence and supervision. In a way, I don't blame them. I once had an Army battalion commander who occasionally tried to "find 500"—meaning that, since he was responsible for 500 officers and soldiers, he wanted to know what any and all of them were doing at a given time. On the surface, he only was trying to get a lesson across regarding accountability of one's troops. But clearly, he saw an important correlation between personnel accessibility and command influence.

Another way to let raw communication overtake the need for meetings is to encourage synchronization. Many times, bosses will call meetings when they perceive that team members are operating on different wavelengths.

Be proactive in ensuring that everybody shares the same information and understands their individual roles in completing a task. You can accomplish this feat by visiting each person concerned with a project and making sure he knows what is expected of him and what others have contributed up to that point. Then you can visit your boss with an appropriate update.

An example: "John, over the weekend, the finishing department ran out of 45-inch pallets for this week's overseas shipment. Tom called to tell me that they used 46-inch pallets instead. This presents a problem because 46-inch pallets don't fit well side-by-side on a sea container. I spoke with Liz. She says 45-inch skids arrive here tomorrow. Greg says he can have the product repacked on the smaller skids by Friday. Sue says we can hold up the shipment until then. I'll keep you posted throughout the week." The shipping team leader has done a couple of smart things by giving his supervisor this briefing. First, he has presented a solution along with the problem (which is a great way to approach any boss with any problem). Second, he has made certain that everybody understands where they all fit into the puzzle. Third, he has been aggressive in keeping his supervisor informed, and he has promised to continue updating. Finally, since everyone seems to be reading from the same sheet of music—and has conveyed that to the boss—he has helped eliminate any inclination his boss may have had to call a meeting.

Do your part to ensure that you and those around you are reading from the same sheet of music, and in the process, keeping your superiors informed.

Incidentally, being aggressive in how you provide information does not have to be limited to projects and problems. Providing information before it's requested is akin to offering spontaneous compliments to people. Periodic blasts of current, useful data tend to knock people off their stride—in a good way. And if they are taken aback by your openness and willingness to share knowledge, it may derail the meeting trains they engineer. Again, meetings never really adequately update managers on what's going on—managers just *think* they do. But if facts are readily available to begin with, the inclination for managers and others to convene meetings is reduced.

What about when information *is* requested and managers are looking for replies to their questions? The key to keeping their concerns from turning into calls for meetings is *response time*. A quick response to requests for data—particularly when it is a habit among coworkers— is the ultimate meeting roadblock. Conversely, if it is the habit of people within an organization to sit on requests for information, meetings will be scheduled simply to mandate a place and a time for the gathering of previously requested reports.

In sum, creating raw communication is a proactive way to convince others not to hold meetings. When people are comfortable with the quality and flow of information around them, they are less likely to call a meeting.

SUMMARY

- Managing without meetings might also mean avoiding the meetings of others and persuading others to hold fewer get-togethers. There are 10 ways to handle people who call meetings:

  1. Stay busy and productive.
  2. Clarify your job description and duties.
  3. Respectfully excuse yourself.

4. Make yourself accessible.

5. Set the example.

6. Obtain the meeting itinerary early and offer answers beforehand.

7. Directly approach someone with your antimeeting philosophy.

8. Voice your displeasure following an unproductive meeting.

9. Refuse offering vehicles of comfort.

10. Assume the role of project manager.

- It is easiest to avoid meetings during a team project by assuming control of the project. Taking on a project also means enjoying the spotlight of success and learning about things outside the normal scope of one's job.

- People are less likely to convene meetings if they perceive an abundance of open communication in their organization.

CHAPTER 10

Know the Ways to Cheat

MAKE SURE THE MEETING IS REALLY UNAVOIDABLE

Everybody cheats when they're dieting. The key to losing weight is to know *how* to cheat. What tastes sweet but doesn't pack a lot of calories? What sticks to your ribs but doesn't have a lot of processed carbohydrates?

The same goes for business-meeting diets. As you strive to make your workday lean and mean, you should know how to indulge the occasional meeting without letting your days become cumbersome once again.

Of course, my argument is that the best meeting is the one not held. But if you *must* hold one, know the ways to cheat your new meeting-less philosophy.

The first step to cheating is determining if the meeting is absolutely unavoidable. There might be times when immediate face-time/real-time interaction between several people at once seems appropriate. Ideally, these encounters are urgent, brief, and not part of a long-term, decision-making process. At times, they might have more to do with allaying the anxiety of a group possessing collective concerns. Or they might serve to appease the herdlike mentality of a particular group. These talks are probably more valuable for advancing the image of a strong, decisive leader than they are for exchanging information and ideas—but that's not a bad thing. When a team perceives its chieftain as valiant and influential, a positive, self-fulfilling prophesy often takes place.

An example of such urgency might be when the team leader has to address an organization in the midst of a crisis. If someone in the group has been injured on the job, or if a company's stock is in the middle of a meltdown, or if a team is weathering cataclysmic changes due to either internal or external forces, the need to bring together lots of familiar faces takes on a soothing appropriateness.

On a less sensational level, sometimes a meeting is unavoidable simply because no other alternative seems fitting. Don't give in immediately to the urge. Contemplate your options and make sure you're not gravitating towards a meeting just because of old habits. And keep in mind before you congregate that there are *lots* of alternatives to consider.

As I solicited success stories for this book, one person's name repeatedly came up: Gus Pagonis, the head of logistics for Sears, Roebuck and Co. "You've *got* to interview Pagonis," said one colleague. "He personifies everything your book is about—hands-on leadership, delegating, and generally just managing by walking around." Walking around—a company the size of Sears?

To be sure, Gus Pagonis, the senior vice president for supply chain management, is a study in streamlined, personal leadership. He gained national attention in 2001 following the terrorist strikes of September 11th. While the supply chains of many companies broke down immediately after the tragedy as transportation was stymied, the supply lines for Sears, under Pagonis's leadership, kept working.

And, yes, he *does* manage a good deal by walking around. He spends about 40 percent of his workweek traveling to Sears distribution centers throughout the country and visiting people at all levels of various operations. One-on-one (sometimes one-on-two) management and mentoring take up another 30 percent. Reporting to colleagues and higher-ups takes up 20 percent. That leaves only 10 percent for convening his own meetings—an astonishingly small amount of time, considering that senior managers statistically spend between one-half and three-quarters of their week in the conference room.

Over the course of a few interviews with Pagonis and two executive members of his team, Tom Coley and Jim Ireland, I found myself listening to managers who had established a systematic way for taking the standard workplace meeting and standing it on its head.

This team does a fine job determining if a meeting is essential by offering a few options in its place. Pagonis has four main ways of interacting with his immediate team, only one of which remotely resembles a typical business meeting. The first method is the bullet in a one-way communiqué that plainly puts forth expectations and *commander's intent.* "There's little need for a meeting if you spell out for people, in writing, exactly what you're looking for," says Pagonis.

The second option is the *three-by-five,* a note with no more information than what one could fit on a three-by-five card. If someone needs direction or feels the need to point out a concern, he sends up a three-by-five. The direction is provided, or the concern is acknowledged and addressed, and the three-by-five is sent back down. If the immediate team leader cannot answer the three-by-five, it gets forwarded to the next level. In the Sears logistics division, three-by-fives pass up and down leadership tiers throughout the day. It's not inconceivable for Pagonis to take delivery of a three-by-five that started with a forklift operator on a loading dock anywhere in the country. He admits that e-mail has largely taken the place of paper three-by-five cards, but these messages still have to follow a strict and concise format. In other words, no dissertations.

The third option is the *stand-up,* a quick meeting where everyone in the room remains standing, offering brief status reports. The meeting often concludes with a pep talk from the team leader.

The fourth option is the *sit-down,* the closest alternative to a traditional meeting. It contains an agenda and involves sitting down and running through more concentrated analyses of subjects.

Why do the *stand-ups* and *sit-downs* take up only one-tenth of Pagonis's time? First, because the stands-ups by their nature take up little time at all. Second, because before a sit-down is scheduled, the information has a chance to work itself through the other three options. If a meeting is avoidable, odds are that these other methods for team connecting will have kept it from happening.

As you contemplate holding a meeting, quickly run through the previous nine chapters of this book and see if you can talk yourself out of it.

1. Are you calling this meeting because you have surrendered to its existence?
2. Do you think the dynamics of your group inherently will keep the meeting from working?
3. Can the meeting be replaced with one-on-one management?
4. Can the meeting be replaced with your strong leadership?
5. Can the meeting be replaced with organizational channeling?
6. Can the meeting be replaced with delegating?
7. Can the meeting be replaced with information or communication technology?
8. Can the meeting be replaced with mentoring?

9. Is the meeting being called by someone else and, if so, can you avoid it without being disrespectful?

If you answer "no" to all nine questions, then perhaps you have reached the point where the meeting is *really* unavoidable.

ENFORCE THE RULES OF ENGAGEMENT

Okay, so now you've done it. You've decided to call a meeting. If you view the standard workplace meeting as the enemy of a productive day (and you should), then basically what you have decided to do is to engage the enemy. Make sure before doing so that you exert some guidelines as you encounter this adversary. Be like General Putnam at the Battle of Bunker Hill, who had an easy enough rule to follow: "Don't one of you fire until you see the whites of their eyes."

The way to cheat your meeting diet is to enforce the rules of engagement as you contemplate, plan, and ultimately convene your meeting.

Here are your rules of engagement.

Restrict your goals and itinerary

Gus Pagonis of Sears argues that the key to any productive meeting is a concise, limited agenda. "The schedule of topics needs to be short and focused," he says. "A meeting that tries to accomplish too many things will end up finishing nothing."

Regional business manager Karen Barry agrees. "You can't try to boil the ocean in one meeting. You need a reasonable agenda that can be discussed and completed in a time frame you have determined."

into *their* level of interest and *their* agenda. Planning and purchasing director John Pastor makes an interesting analogy. "It's like football," he says. "The quarterback is worried about the next play, the coach is worried about the next game, and the general manager is worried about the next season. So why should all three of them be in a room at once?" Such multitiered inviting has another bad effect: it takes important people away from their jobs. "It's like the general manager of the team pulling the coach and the quarterback into a meeting while the game's going on," says Pastor.

In a sense, that's what some managers do every day.

Set a time limit

As you consider your goals and your itinerary, visualize how the discussion will take place, how abruptly you might be able to wrap it up, and how quickly the decision makers might be able to offer a resolution. Write down the number of minutes for each topic and add them up. That's your time limit—ideally no more than 20 minutes to an hour.

A time limit is even better if it's not a round number of minutes. Process improvement director John Frost suggests that a meeting doesn't need to be a full hour long just because today's scheduling software leans people towards 60-minute intervals. "Why block out an hour?" he asks rhetorically. "If your agenda focuses on four key things and you think you can address each item in 10 minutes, then plan the meeting for 40 minutes." Frost says he enjoys setting an amount of time for a meeting and then attempting to finish early. "It's a game I play," he says, "trying to be that one person who completes a meeting in *less* time than was allocated."

Visualize yourself running through your agenda. Do you see yourself attaining your goals? How do you see yourself doing it? Jot a few ideas down on paper, contemplate them, and then circle the one or two things that strike you as the most viable. Put them in order. Spell out on paper how you're going to broach each topic and what questions you're going to ask of your team.

Your goals and itinerary are set.

Limit your invitation list

When preparing for the unavoidable meeting, make sure you invite only those people who absolutely have to be there. If you are not the only decision maker, then having all of them at your meeting is essential. As Tom Coley of Sears logistics notes, "There's no point to the meeting if the decision makers aren't on hand."

Also, consider inviting people who will contribute several different views to the same issue. Says Pagonis: "In a meeting, it's best to be surrounded by people who are going to disagree with you. If you find yourself in a room with total, harmonious consensus, you probably haven't given the topic full consideration."

Don't overinvite. There's a natural tendency towards bringing everyone remotely affected by a decision into a discussion. Limit your meeting to your key players and the decision makers.

Also, avoid the overinviting that comes about when you call on people too high up or too far down from your echelon of decision making. The danger is that you will have people around that can't relate to the resolution at hand. And if people can't relate, they have one of two choices: a) sit around uninterested, or b) try to pull the meeting

Be prepared

Packaging and shipping supervisor John Decker suggests that the best host of a meeting is a prepared host. "Review your points in advance before gathering your team," he says. "Have your homework done. Be ready to make it work."

Decker also suggests that a well-prepared meeting is best scheduled for early in the day or in the shift, when people are fresh and not concentrating on lunch or quitting time. There's no sense taking the time to plan a meeting for people who aren't paying attention.

Preparation also includes sharing the agenda with people ahead of time. That way, they are able to attend the meeting with a topic already researched and pondered. They are able to offer solutions that make sense, rather than shoot from the hip. Furthermore, if half a dozen people come to your meeting with half a dozen different solutions, the potential for groupthink is not as great. There's no guarantee that a bad idea won't take over the room anyway, but at least it won't be for lack of other opinions.

What is an appropriate amount of notice? It depends on the urgency of the topic and the ability of your attendees to produce educated answers.

There are three more rules of engagement: *Keep it short and focused; follow your agenda with a vengeance;* and *don't let the meeting run you.* Let's look at these last three rules in detail.

Keep it short and focused

Special Operations commander Ron Green has found a way to keep meetings capped at 25 minutes. He schedules them to begin exactly 25 minutes before morning physical training. "With over 100 soldiers waiting for morning PT, there's no pontificating," says Green. He calls his brief meetings "shoot-outs," where his small group of officers comes prepared to focus on big issues, ask important questions, and provide researched answers. And if the whirlwind agenda isn't accomplished in 25 minutes, too bad. Morning calisthenics are calling!

Green understands human nature and the human tendency to ramble if time constraints are yielding. He simply doesn't give himself the chance to schmooze: his boundaries are inflexible. In order to keep your meeting short and focused, consider scheduling it in such a manner that it *must* start on time and it simply *cannot* run over the allotted time. Back its scheduled conclusion right up against another calendared event, as long as it's not another meeting. An example might be conducting a meeting just before a series of machines are to be reprogrammed or recalibrated. If large groups of people are sitting around waiting for something constructive to get started, you have no choice but to wrap up your get-together. Feel pressured? Good. You should.

Jump right into the topic at hand. There's no time for coffee and donuts. There's no time to talk about last night's big game on television. There's no time for company rumors and no time for nicey-nice social-izing. Assume control from the minute you have a quorum and never let go of that control.

Again, my argument is that meetings across the board should be done away with in favor of methods that better reflect human nature and the way we interact. But wouldn't the meetings we suffer through be so much easier to handle if they simply started on time and began with something productive at the outset? If you must hold a meeting, hit the ground running.

As you begin your conference, spell out precisely what needs to get done and the amount of time it's going to take. Announce the topics and the goals. Tell people how the time breaks down for each topic. Let them know how long each person is allowed to speak.

At some point, they should know that the discussion will cease and decisions, if necessary, will be rendered. If you are not the decision maker, let the decision maker know when you will be calling on her for a course of action. Make no bones about wanting answers and wanting them fast. If you have given an ample amount of notice to those in attendance, and if they have done their homework before showing up, the answers won't be forced or haphazard.

As you watch the clock, go ahead and *really* watch the clock. If there's not one in the place you're meeting, there ought to be. A big clock with a giant sweeping second hand should be the comoderator of your meeting.

If there is no clock, or if the clock is in an awkward place for you to keep checking (such as behind you, where you would have to turn away rudely from people while they're talking), then you should consider bringing your own. A small, battery-powered, nonticking clock placed on the conference table might not be accessible to all (since it will be facing towards you), but it certainly will send the message that you mean business about keeping things on track. I personally don't recommend anything that beeps or chirps or otherwise marks 5 or 10-minute intervals. You don't want to cross the boundary from being purposeful into being just plain obnoxious.

Having said that, the most important and perhaps most uncomfortable role you'll play in keeping the meeting short and focused is that of time enforcer. It's tough knowing when to cut people off and knowing how to do it without being too abrasive. Again, if you let people know up front how much time is apportioned for discussion, then there shouldn't be too much of a surprise when you politely ask someone to surrender the floor and move on to the next person or the next topic.

Considering the confidence level and self-pride that your key people are sure to possess, cutting them off might be a bit of a chore. The mix of personalities in any room suggests that your limits and your authority might be challenged. That's just one of the many games people play and one of the many reasons that meetings stink. Stick to your guns and keep things zeroed in on the goals you announced at commencement of the gathering.

You might want to consider assigning the role of enforcer to someone else. NTP Software CEO Bruce Backa suggests that the meeting's timeline should be written down and followed like a script and that perhaps someone other than the moderator be assigned to follow the timeline. The enforcer calls out when topic discussions are to be concluded or when key decisions are to be decided upon.

Your meeting should stay on a fast, consistent pace. There should be a high level of energy and a sense of momentum in the room. Under your guidance, people should feel energetic and—depending on the topic—even enthused during the discussion. There should be an electric crackle in the air as you move from topic to topic and decision to decision. People should sense that this is not a standard workplace meeting unless, that is, you've developed such a knack for this kind of conference that people have become used to your vigorous and productive stride.

And if people *have* become accustomed to the way you control these talks, the enthusiasm might feed on itself. That is, if people know their time is not going to be wasted, they might show up eager and prepped for the "shoot-out."

Nothing can derail a meeting faster than someone attempting to spin the conversation onto a different topic. An example:

Moderator: "There's a glitch in the software that needs to be isolated and patched."

Key person: "That software never should have been purchased in the first place, and let me tell you why." And a long dissertation ensues.

Stay on the topic. Graciously suggest to the person that his discussion on software packages already purchased and in use needs to take place another time. Perhaps you can schedule a time for that discussion right then, and make it a one-on-one discussion between him and the person who decides on software contracts. (Is it you?) And then move on.

Remember that people often have personal agendas. Sometimes the agenda is nothing more than wanting to be noticed or respected. At times, a person's agenda might simply involve wanting to be disruptive. Who knows? You can be a psychologist later. For now, keep the meeting moving along.

Scheduling time for side topics should not just be a way of dealing with unruly people. Clearly, any thoughtful discussion is going to produce concerns and issues that fall outside the scope of that particular get-together. The way you acknowledge those topics and the professionalism of people who bring them up is to keep a notepad on the table and take notes as the discussion goes on. Put a star by points needing addressing. Throughout the meeting, openly state any new, unresolved issues that have been put on the table. Schedule one-on-ones between yourself and the key people who can address these topics. Perhaps you can schedule time for two key people to hook up with each other.

An important note: don't suggest that you meet with someone directly after the meeting. Yes, the one-on-one time directly after a conference is often the time when the most gets done. But that predicament only reflects the power of one-on-one interaction; it doesn't support the idea of smaller meetings following larger meetings. Besides, if someone is being brash during your conference, he shouldn't be rewarded with more time afterward.

Throughout the encounter, keep things mission oriented and goal oriented. People should feel an underlying sense of purpose in the room. They should be persuaded by an undercurrent of urgency and the need for accomplishment. They should be swept away by the meeting's brevity and its laser-beam point of convergence. There should never be the sentiment that a meeting is being held for its own sake. The mission should always be like another person in the room.

Follow your agenda with a vengeance

Hey, it's just a short meeting with one or two points. It will be over with in no time. Why not just wing it?

The answer is that the less scripted a conference is, the more likely it is to fall prey to the flawed nature of people. Make sure you put together an agenda that breaks everything down to 5-minute blocks. If you plan a 20-minute meeting, then four specific, 5-minute outcomes should occur. For an hour-long meeting, a sequence of 12 different minievents should take place.

And then follow your agenda with a vengeance.

Gus Pagonis of Sears has a specific format for each of his four types of management communication: *bulletin, three-by-five, stand-up*, and *sit-down*. Within his schedule of weekly sit-downs, he breaks down the classifications and agendas even further. For example, one type of sit-down is the relatively traditional staff call. The staff call script calls for each department head to provide three "ups" (good things that the department has accomplished), three "downs" (problems or things that need attention, with solutions in progress or under consideration), and items of interest (matters pertinent to the group and circumstances that are upcoming). People are strongly encouraged not to stray from the format. Says team member Jim Ireland: "People know that if they don't each offer three department 'downs,' they might be embarrassed by having them provided."

Pagonis rejects the notion of free-form meetings and the alleged creativity they're supposed to bring about. "No one has ever proven to me the benefit of having people sit together in a room and haphazardly brainstorm," he says.

Clearly, his methods hearken back to the *freedom in structure* philosophy, where the more defined the rules are, the more inventive people will be in finding solutions within given parameters. The idea of people randomly tossing out ideas that are placed without criticism onto large sheets of papers *seems* freewheeling, resourceful, and perhaps even synergistic. But without the road ahead clearly mapped, such abstraction ultimately fails to harness useful innovations.

How else can you ensure that your agenda will be respected and followed? Tom Coley of the Sears logistics team suggests that you can establish your authority in the room just by forcing the meeting to start on time. "People don't like waiting," he says, "but most of them have come to accept it. I recommend that as long as the decision makers are present, you should set a commanding tone right away by getting things started promptly."

Coley also offers that you should try to remain the focus of attention by not having physical diversions around. "People love charts these days," he says. "But colorful charts can easily take people's concentration away from what you're trying to say."

Your authority might be boosted by having an attack dog around. Again, I like Bruce Backa's idea of having someone on hand specifically to look at the clock, enforce the script, and cut people off when they stray from the timeline or the topic. Without having to tend to such housekeeping, you can concentrate on what matters. Also, by adding a layer between you and the person most likely to throw a meeting off track, you create a buffer that allows you to maintain an air of control (while someone else has to play bad guy).

As you follow your agenda, keep your eye on the brass ring. Assess each phase of your timeline for how much closer it's bringing you to your objective.

For example, suppose your company makes a product that winds up having a defect—perhaps a defect caught by your company's corporate head of quality control. The next day at work, concern has turned into panic, and then panic into hysteria. After running several antimeeting options through your head, you decide that, considering the circumstances, it is best to pull your team into a room and ease everyone's fears. As with some meetings that seem appropriate to the normally meeting-less manager, this get-together tends to serve your unadvertised goals of addressing urgency and portraying decisive leadership.

The meeting, scheduled for 20 minutes, begins promptly. You spend the first 5 minutes reviewing what the director of quality is saying. You spend the next 5 minutes covering your office's response and the actions it's taking to repair the defect or replace the faulty items. You take the next 5 minutes to remind people that you have been through such dips in the road before and that everything eventually turned out okay. You then announce that you will answer questions for the next 5 minutes. At the 20-minute mark, you emphasize your faith in the team. The meeting ends as punctually as it began.

During each of the four phases, you need to access your team's response to the information and guidance you're putting out. Perhaps at this high level of anxiety, you are able to get the attention of more than 3 of 10 people. Perhaps a connection is being made. As you make these split-second assessments, bear in mind the underlying goals: alleviating internal apprehension and projecting strong guidance.

A concluding item to any agenda should be determining if any follow-up is necessary. If your quick appraisals indicate that the goals have been met, you're finished. If you sense that information was not received, or received unfavorably, you may need to schedule supplementary one-on-one communication or perhaps even (gulp!) another meeting. If your goal was to reach a decision or a course of action, and nothing was decided upon, then you need to arrange another meeting with at least the decision makers on hand.

Don't extend the meeting, thinking that a few more minutes might attain whatever was missed. Whatever dynamics kept you from achieving your goal are still going on in the room. It's better to reschedule. Besides, by refusing to extend a meeting, you're sending an appropriate message that you follow an agenda with a vengeance.

And the final agenda item: end the meeting promptly and clear the room. After all, your group's time is expensive. "Never forget that it costs money to have people in a conference room," Bruce Backa says. "The time invested in a meeting is no different than the money spent on a project. Once you've exceeded your planned investment, you'd better be ready to cut the meeting off or experience a resource loss instead of a profit."

Don't let the meeting run you

As you conduct the unavoidable meeting, make sure that you don't find yourself losing control or perhaps *being* controlled by what's happening in the conference room.

Aside from following a tight agenda, there are ways to make sure the meeting doesn't take on a life of its own.

Once again, there's something to be said for having around only those people who directly impact or are directly impacted by the decision at hand. Expanding the roster any further exposes the meeting to personal agendas and irrelevant input. Keep it limited to your key players and experts for making decisions. Keep information or motivational get-togethers restricted to the people who most need to hear what's getting put out.

Sear's Jim Ireland has a good way to keep things from spiraling out of control. He says, "As a meeting is wrapping up, don't ever ask, 'Does anyone have anything else?'" Sure, if everyone's together, the natural propensity is to ask for any new items that might affect the group. But if the agenda is complete and your schedule has people moving towards the door, why subject everyone to a new set of issues? "You're just opening a new can of worms," states Ireland. Perhaps it's better to reward the group for sticking with the agenda by allowing them their freedom.

Early on, I noted that some of the best ideas get communicated during the one-on-ones that immediately follow a meeting—and for good reason. Due to many of the circumstances we've covered up to this point, people with the best solutions often wait until after a meeting is finished and then allow the principles of one-on-one management to work for them. However, there's a big problem with following such a sequence. The time for one-on-one communication is *not* in the conference room directly following a meeting. If you *must* hold a meeting, then hold a meeting. If you prefer to communicate one-on-one, then communicate one-on-one. But don't follow one with the other. Here's why.

Suppose you have determined that a meeting is necessary, and your key people have just formed a decision in a conference room. As such, the decision should hold water. It should have a certain finality and strength to it. Within the organization, this important judgment should carry as a rule of law. But suppose immediately after the decision-making meeting, a key person approaches you, one-on-one, and offers you new, pertinent information and a new, applicable solution? Hasn't that person just undermined the meeting? If other key people are involved, aren't you now obligated to call them back into *another* meeting?

Gus Pagonis suggests people be informed up front that when the meeting is over, the decision is final. "People should leave a meeting with their marching orders," he says. "The last thing you need after a meeting is a bunch of ideas still floating around among hangers-on."

One final thought on your unavoidable meeting. It's avoidable.

Yes, we just went over some anomalous scenarios where a meeting seems essential. And we covered some rules of engagement for keeping things on track and avoiding the pitfalls of human tendencies. But after all is said and done and analyzed, you should still assume the attitude that the best meeting is the one not called. Forcing people to share real time is a time drain and a financial drain on your team. The goals of a meeting are rarely met. Conference room dynamics will always include colorful personalities and hidden, personal agendas. And, due to human nature, your flawed meeting never *really* can be fixed. The most you can hope for is to stumble onto the perfect solution by using a far-less-than-perfect vehicle for finding it.

Instead, allow me to suggest a healthy menu of alternatives. Discover one-on-one management. Become a stronger team leader. Learn the process of organizational channeling. Improve your delegating skills. Use technology to communicate. Try mentoring. And, while you're at it, set the example and influence the meeting tendencies of others.

SUMMARY

- A manager should determine if a meeting is absolutely necessary by weighing it against other available options.

- The manager who decides a meeting is unavoidable should follow rules of engagement:

  1. Restrict your goals and itinerary.

  2. Limit your invitation list.

3. Set a time limit.

4. Be prepared.

5. Keep it short and focused.

6. Follow your agenda with a vengeance.

7. Don't let the meeting run you.

- A manager should live by the creed that the best meeting is the one not called.

Accept the Challenge!

The world is going to hell in a business meeting. The statistics are pretty clear-cut. Today's managers spend between one-quarter and three-quarters of their workday attending meetings. At least half of all meeting time is unproductive if not destructive. And the problem, by most accounts, is getting worse.

This assault on managers' time (not to mention the time of everybody in attendance) has been mounting for at least the last two decades, as participative management models have made their way into everyday corporate practice. Many of today's companies follow *work team* concepts, communal quality controls and group problem-solving techniques. Everybody seems to have their say at once, and meetings abound.

Let's do some math. In the United States, there are about 40 million people stating their occupations as managerial and professional, with an additional 39 million people falling under the employment categories of technical, sales, and administrative support. If, on average, managers and administrators spend half of an eight-hour day in meetings, and if about half of that time is wasted, then two hours per person per day are lost. That's 158 million lost work hours per day in the United States alone—or about 38 *billion* lost hours per year! Imagine what this number would grow to if we were to include the hours consumed by nonmanagement people pulled into these useless meetings.

Yes, the amount of collectively wasted time and lost opportunity in any organization on any given workday due to meetings is staggering—and yet somehow accepted. We hate meetings, but we surrender to them, accepting them as the unfortunate way that managers manage. We have been conditioned as people to embrace the common management concepts in use and accept meetings for the flawed vehicles that they are.

Is there a different way for managers to conduct their lives at work? Is it possible to run an office or enterprise without meetings and to elude the meetings of others?

Absolutely!

The notion of a meeting-free workday may be revolutionary, but the methods described in this book are not extreme. I have spent years watching and conversing with successful managers who avoid the trappings of business meetings to the benefit of themselves and their organizations. I submit to you that truly futuristic leaders should dedicate themselves to a life without meetings.

In Chapter 9 of this text, I suggest 10 ways to avoid the meetings of others. Allow me to offer an eleventh. Place a copy of this book on the desk of someone who holds too many business meetings. I compare this action to anonymously placing breath mints on the desk of someone with halitosis. If you have bosses or coworkers who unwittingly waste other people's time by calling meetings, why not stealthily provide them a copy of this book? They might see a new light on the horizon and discover how meetings have been hurting rather than helping them.

There is a not-too-distant place in our world where people are allowed to carry out their work as individuals. A place where information and work effort are successfully harvested. A place where everyone in an organization feels involved and helpful. A place where group synergy regularly takes place. All without conference room get-togethers. Let's get off this crazy carnival ride we call a *business meeting* and head for that place. Let's begin more productive, professional lives.

Let's accept the challenge!

Scott Snair

Notes

CHAPTER 1

The uncomfortable statistic that managers spend about half of their workday in meetings has been conjectured and referred to for some time. The calculation has been asserted for over 40 years in meeting guru Frank Snell's classic text, *How to Hold a Better Meeting* (New York: Cornerstone Library, 1959, reprinted 1979).

In Paul R. Timm's book, *How to Hold Successful Meetings* (Franklin Lakes, New Jersey: Career Press, 1997), Snell is referenced as saying higher-level executives spend more than 75 percent of their day in the conference room. Timm also argues that meeting time overall has increased in recent years.

The concept of *groupthink*—where bad decisions are made by team members preoccupied with conforming—was revealed and exhaustively investigated in the 1970s and 1980s by Irving L. Janis. His most celebrated book on the subject is *Victims of Groupthink: A Psychological Study of Foreign Policy Decisions and Fiascoes* (Boston: Houghton Mifflin, 1972). A second, revised edition that includes a discussion of the Watergate cover-up was published in 1983.

The corrupt plans conceived during meetings in the Nixon White House are well detailed by Michael A. Genovese in his book, *The Watergate Crisis: Greenwood Press Guides to the Historic Events of the Twentieth Century* (Westport, Connecticut: Greenwood Press, 1999). Genovese selects many revealing excerpts from now-public, taped conversations that demonstrate how a deplorable idea can grip a conforming group.

The disastrous Bay of Pigs decision-making processes that took place during Cabinet meetings in the Kennedy Administration are covered extensively in Grayston L. Lynch's *Decision for Disaster: Betrayal at the Bay of Pigs* (Washington, DC: Brassey's, 1998).

Abraham Maslow was a forerunner of humanistic psychology in the 1940s and 1950s. His famous Theory of Motivation and Hierarchy of Human Needs were unique at the time in that they touched on psychology as it affects everyone—rather than focusing on psychoses. He carried his theories into the business world and promoted the possibilities leaders can achieve when they accept the human side of both themselves and the people they manage. My favorite Maslow book is his biography, *The Right to be Human: A Biography of Abraham Maslow* (Los Angeles: Tarcher/New York: St. Martin's Press, 1988), by Edward Hoffman.

CHAPTER 2

A detailed analysis of the mind games people play on the golf course can be found in Bruce Ollstein's book, *Combat Golf: The Competitor's Field Manual for Winning Against Any Opponent* (New York: Viking, 1996). Ollstein does a fine job defining golf as, well, war. He documents the various, subtle psychological maneuvers golfers use and how they are applied.

CHAPTER 3

The Rogerian method of active listening, what Carl R. Rogers calls "the reflection of attitudes," is covered in his counseling classic, *Client-Centered Therapy* (New York: Houghton Mifflin, 1951).

CHAPTER 4

The sobering Yale studies on the human tendency to follow authority are recounted in-depth by Stanley Milgram, who conducted the research in the 1960s. His book is *Obedience to Authority: An Experimental View (1st ed.)* (New York: Harper & Row, 1974).

Aside from being stirred by my personal experiences and interviews, the idea that self-managed work teams harm individuality is inspired in part by Stanley M. Herman's great book, *A Force of Ones: Reclaiming Individual Power in a Time of Teams, Work Groups and Other Crowds (1st ed.)* (San Francisco: Jossey-Bass, 1994). Herman says it all when he argues that groups simply can't be inventive or courageous—only individuals can. I am especially impressed by the refreshing boldness of this book, published during the mid-1990s when team-building models were in their heyday at many corporations.

The topics of the Equity Theory of motivation and *transactional versus transformational* leadership are expounded in my favorite college textbook ever, *A Primer on Organizational Behavior (3rd ed.)* (New York: Wiley, 1994), by James L. Bowditch and Anthony F. Buono. The textbook's fourth edition came out in 1996. The fifth edition was published in 2000.

The phrases "seek responsibility and take responsibility for their actions" and, later on, "seek responsibility and take responsibility" are drawn from West Point's 11 Principles of Leadership. I always considered the third principle, *Seek responsibility and take responsibility for your actions*, one of the most important ones—and the most difficult one to follow in this age of blame and victimization. I looked up these principles in my pocket-sized *Bugle Notes (76th Volume)* (West Point,

New York: U.S. Military Academy, 1984), presented by the Academy's Staff of 1984 and kept within reach by all cadets in my class.

CHAPTER 5

The poem, "The Blind Men and the Elephant" was John Godfrey Saxe's famous effort in putting an old "Hindoo [sic] fable" to rhyme. The poem appears in many places. I found it in an old, dusty volume called *The Poetical Work of John Godfrey Saxe* (New York: Houghton Mifflin, 1882).

The surveying of 56 managers was conducted in 2000. I asked them individually to review the doctrine of organizational channeling. Hoping for genuine feedback, I initially misled them to believe the method was conceived by someone else and had been around for a few years.

Feedback was largely positive, with several managers offering supporting anecdotes. The misgivings of others, however, were pointed—and are excerpted and addressed in Chapter 5.

The second Principle of Leadership, *Be technically and tactically proficient,* is quoted from *Bugle Notes (76th Volume)* (West Point, New York: US Military Academy, 1984), previously mentioned.

CHAPTER 6

My favorite book on delegating is Dale D. McConkey's *No-Nonsense Delegation (Revised ed.)* (New York: AMACOM, 1986). It's a wonderful text for helping a manager to plan and control delegating and to develop and evaluate subordinates.

CHAPTER 7

Kimball Fisher and Mareen Duncan Fisher's book is *The Distributed Mind: Achieving High Performance Through the Collective Intelligence of Knowledge Work Teams* (New York: AMACOM, 1998). While I admittedly do not subscribe to all of the book's tenets, I am fascinated with Fisher and Fisher's discussion on leaders becoming "boundary managers," and with their description of cyberorganizations and virtual knowledge teams. Their most recent book on distance technology and distance management is *The Distance Manager: A Hands-On Guide to Managing Off-Site Employees and Virtual Teams* (New York: McGraw-Hill, 2000).

CHAPTER 10

More on Gus Pagonis's management style can be found in his rousing leadership book. The text is *Moving Mountains: Lessons in Leadership and Logistics from the Gulf War* (Boston: Harvard Business School Press, 1992), by William G. Pagonis with Jeffrey L. Cruikshank.

If you *must* hold a meeting, I recommend Michael Doyle and David Straus's book *How to Make Meetings Work* (New York: Berkley, 1976, reprinted 1993). There is Paul R. Timm's handy text, *How to Hold Successful Meetings* (Franklin Lakes, New Jersey: Career Press, 1997). I also like the advice regarding meetings in Bob Nelson and Peter Economy's *Managing for Dummies* (New York: Hungry Minds, 1999). And, of course, there are a number of books by Frank Snell, including his timeless work, *How to Hold a Better Meeting* (New York: Cornerstone Library, 1959, reprinted 1979).

CONCLUSION

The statistic that half of all meeting time is unproductive is a commonly accepted figure. (As you might expect, I think the proportion is much higher.) Most recently, Nelson and Economy state in their book *Managing for Dummies*—previously mentioned—that studies have dialed in the uselessness percentage to a more exact 53 percent.

The statement that the problem of meetings is getting worse is based on anecdotal evidence and on Paul R. Timm's written observations, previously mentioned.

The demographics regarding occupations are taken from the U.S. Department of Commerce's *Statistical Abstract of the United States: 2000 (120th ed.)* (Washington, D.C.: U.S. Census Bureau, 2000).

Index

About the Author

Scott Snair is a West Point graduate and president of his class. His distinguished military career included service as a cannon platoon leader in Operation Desert Storm. Shifting gears into the private sector, he has worked in sales, manufacturing, and logistics management with companies such as Verizon and International Paper. He currently serves as an academic administrator with Seton Hall University's Stillman School of Business and as a consultant/lecturer. Contact Scott at www.StopTheMeeting.com.